There Is Still Love

There Is Still Love

MALACHI MARTIN

CARMEL • NEW YORK 10512

Copyright © 1984 by Malachi Martin.
This edition published by arrangement with
Ballantine Books, a division of Random House, Inc.

Macmillan Publishing Company
866 Third Avenue, New York, N.Y. 10022
Collier Macmillan Canada, Inc.

Library of Congress Cataloging in Publication Data
Martin, Malachi.
There is still love.
1. Love (Theology) I. Title.
BV4639.M326 1984   241'.4   83-25642
ISBN 0-02-580440-5

10 9 8 7 6 5 4 3 2 1

Designed by Jack Meserole

Printed in the United States of America

This Guideposts edition is published by special arrangement
with Macmillan Publishing Company.

The first portions of the scenarios in this book are based upon true incidents. They have been chosen because they embody behavior and attitudes that are in many ways hallmarks of life in our times, and because they demonstrate dramatically some of the most common and profound misunderstandings concerning Christian love. All names and places and many other elements as well have been changed. Any similarity to actual persons living or dead is unintentional and purely coincidental.

CONTENTS

There Is Still Love

Is There Still Love?

It was getting into the late evening, but the five of us sitting there in the warm glow of the lamplight hardly noticed. Dinner, given for an old and good friend—Margaret, as I call her here—who was in town on a business trip, was long since over, but the talk went on easily, as it does among old friends.

It must have been near midnight when the conversation took a special turn. I'm not even sure now how it came up. Oh, we had noticed the change. Margaret had aways been so easy and bright and sure in everything. But now there seemed a strain, a sadness about her. You couldn't quite put your finger on it, and no one had asked her what was the matter.

Margaret had spent most of her adult life, perhaps thirty years in all, working hard and with deep devotion, for one company. She had grown to become one of the best in her field in the whole country, even as the company itself had doubled and redoubled its prestige and success with the passage of the years. Still, as hard and demanding as Margaret's work had been, there had always been pleasure and satisfaction, too. Service and excellence had been the watchwords by which my old friend and her employer had lived and done business. There had always been the sure sense of people caring about people, about what they did, about how they went about it.

"If we were fair and did our work with a sense of respect and accomplishment," Margaret told us that night, "we had faith that the success and the profit would grow like a plant that's watered and fed. But it was more than that. For us, profit and success included something else. What we did didn't just make us a little richer in money. It gave us some real happiness. There was always a fullness in our daily lives we wouldn't have had otherwise."

That's the way it had all been for her, until the very success and respect that Margaret and her colleagues had achieved made her company the prime target for a takeover by a group of what she accurately, if bitterly, described as "bottom-line managers," people whose sole interest was profit, and whose sole meaning for that word was money.

The takeover of her company was successful. We all read about it in the papers. What we hadn't known, what you almost never read about in the papers, was what Margaret told us now. The new managers wanted what devotion had built. But they quickly set about tearing out the heart of what had made it all work, what had made the company so attractive for them in the first place.

"It's like a great betrayal," Margaret told us, a new bitterness in her voice. Past service and merit counted for nothing now. New people were brought in from "headquarters." Old employees were fired or shunted aside to hang on the best way they could, or to leave. Employees close to retirement were special targets, because bottom-line managers don't like to pay pensions.

And who cared? Service, customers, devotion, loyalty—none of that mattered any more. Caring and fairness were replaced in almost no time by something else, something impersonal and coarse, something without heart and without responsibility—*human* responsibility. Margaret pronounced that word "human" with an emphasis that still echoes in my memory.

"Just get the bucks!" Margaret mimicked the new motto for her company. "And let everything else go hang!" Then she turned to me. Her face wasn't angry, but terribly sad, and I was sure there were tears at the back of her eyes. "What happened to caring in this country?" Her question was almost a whisper. "Whatever happened to love?"

It sounds familiar, doesn't it? In fact too familiar. That wasn't the first time I'd heard that sad question in one form or another, and it would not be the last. I hear it almost every day from one person or another. Everyone I speak to has heard it, or thought it, or even asked it.

People at work leave their benches or their desks or their boardrooms and shake their heads at the coldness they find invading everywhere, trying to figure out what's wrong, wondering if anyone ever cares anymore. Parents look at their children, husbands and wives at one another, and ask silently or out loud: What went wrong? Friends gather at parties, and the young and not-so-young fling themselves into the mindless noise of discos and bars and, as though all alone, nearly weep as they wonder where the warmth, the caring they came looking for, could possibly have gone. Commuters listen to the radio or read the morning news, and it's all about a John Hinckley who says he shot to kill for "love" of a girl he'd never even met; or about a man who shot the Pope in the midst of Love's blessing, "to make the world a better place"; or about a man who committed rape, or one of a hundred twisted, violent turnabouts of love that scream out at us—often in blood—from the streets of our cities and towns. Sometime during nearly every day, something almost always happens that forces us to ask, "Is there still love?" And no one ever thinks anymore that it's an odd question.

So absent does love seem from our lives, that a kind of bitter, upside down humor has crept into our everyday language, and we begin to wonder if a lot of us haven't just given up. All of us talk about the lethal, mind-degrading drug, PCP, as "angel dust." We don't even shudder at the implied sacrilege. A nuclear-tipped rocket carried under each wing of our latest warplane is familiarly called a "bucketful of sunshine" by the pilots trained to press that particular button. Bitter, cynical descriptions are everywhere. They seem to bare ugly teeth at us and say: "There are no angels. There will be no sunshine. There is no love."

We may not be able to say exactly what the mentality is of those who coin that language. But we feel the pain of something profoundly wrong. And the pain is only deepened by the fact that we accept it all.

What's happened, then? After all, most of us seem to remember a time when it was different, a time when, rich or poor, love and caring did enrich our lives. Is there something new in our world? Something so terrible that we are hypnotized into silence and acquiescence by it? Something that's never been here before, and so eludes all of our strategies for coping with it? Or has Love really turned its back on us? Has Love really gone away?

The answer to those questions is No. There is nothing in our world that hasn't been here almost since the start of it all. Love has always been here, and always will be, because love is of God. And betrayal of love has been here for almost as long: from that first arrogant cry of a loveless Archangel, "No! I will not serve!" flung in the face of Love; to Adam, refusing to obey his loving Creator; to Cain, drowning love in the blood of his brother Abel; to Joseph, betrayed by his jealous brothers; to Absalom, trampling on the love of David; to Judas, betraying Love Itself with the sacred sign of love, the kiss; and beyond that, down through all the ages, into this, our time of "angel dust." Love and the loyalty of love. Hate and its betrayal of love.

No, nothing essential has changed. There have always been the come-hither antics of wealth and power posing as comely substitutes for love. One way or another, there have always been bottom-line ethics and make-it-now morality. And there have always been the purely here-and-now remedies for our groaning spirits. Yet, for all the appeal of social and political "solutions," Love isn't voted in or out of office every four or eight years. It doesn't depend on popularity polls or corporate promotions or expensive clothes. It doesn't come because you're wearing a new pair of tight-cut designer pants and a silk shirt—or because you aren't. Love never changes. And it never has, since men like Abraham and Moses and David and John and Paul spoke with Love Itself, and then turned to us and told us about it. It has never changed, not even from before the time when those men walked upon the Earth. The

voice of love is as present and as stunning and as transforming for every person who hears it and listens to what it
has to say, as ever it was.

That night, during the conversation after dinner, what
I heard in my friend Margaret's question was more than
just "Is there still love?" What I heard was a plea, a demand, even. It was as if my friend was giving an ultimatum to God: "If there is no love for me in this life,
then it would be better if my life ended. Let there be no
mistake. I mean: Love! And I mean: For me! And I mean:
Here and now in this ordinary life of mine!

"Friendship? Fine! Respect? Success? Acquaintance?
Security? Loyalty? Fine! All of these are fine, even necessary. But without love they simply aren't enough. Love in
general, whatever that means, or even love once lived and
then lost, is not enough. And the promise of love-in-the-sky-
when-I-die is not enough to carry me through this life."

That ultimatum isn't new to God, either. Margaret
wasn't the first one to make it. And God has answered it.
For Margaret and for each one of us. Not with thunder
that drowns out every other sound, or with lightning that
shoots across the heavens and blinds the eye to everything
else. Nothing so spectacular. Nothing so easy. Nothing so
obvious. Nothing that means you don't have to put something into it, too. Nothing that means you don't have to
make a choice. That's the way it is with him: He takes the
first step, but you have to take the next one.

What he did was this: He simply made us his, all over
again. Just as he always said he would. He gave us his son.
He walked with ordinary men and women who were just
like you and me. And he told those men and women, and
told us, about loyalty and success and Caesar and about his

Father. He told us about all the things my friend talked about that night—hope and betrayal and perseverance—and all the things other friends, yours and mine, talk about all the time. He told about marriage and friendship and adultery and infidelity. He told us about children and parents and ministers and priests and sinners and saints and Heaven and Hell.

And he told us about love. Especially, he told us about love. At the very end of his life on this earth, a time when each of us says what is most important to us and what we most want to impress on those we dearly care for and are leaving behind—he told us then, again and again, about love.

"As the Father has loved me," Jesus said only hours before his death, mindful of his betrayal and his coming crucifixion, "so I have loved you. Live on in my love. You will live in my love, if you keep my commandments, even as I have kept my Father's commandments. All this I tell you so that my joy may be yours, and your joy may be complete. This is my commandment to you: Love one another, as I have loved you."

Powerful words! Even two thousand years later they make us yearn.

But, after all, isn't this another day? God doesn't speak now the way he did in "Bible days." And, back then, there weren't bloodless banks and smelly, crazy bag-ladies, nuclear bombs, and insane men running the world, men ready to blow us to smithereens in the name of peace and freedom from this or that or who-cares-what! And there wasn't this confusion. I mean, nowadays, Trinity is as likely to mean that site in New Mexico where they tested the first atom bomb, as it is to mean the great God in his eternal mystery. And "good will" is an item on an accountant's balance sheet when one company is about to take over another one, not that special grace the angel sang about in the skies above Bethlehem where the baby and his mother had taken refuge that first Christmas night.

I mean, you have to admit it! Just look around. It's not just what we say. It's what we do. Things are different now! Everyone is living with everyone else, and hardly anyone bothers with marriage. And nearly half of the ones who do, get divorced anyway. And the parents fight over children like cattle or something. "Mister," a cab driver told me recently, "I could tell you stories! It just isn't the same anymore."

Isn't it? Could that cab driver tell me any stories I haven't heard? More important, could he tell me any stories Jesus hasn't heard? Because, after all, love is *his* promise. *He* guarantees it.

Yet, there seems to be a condition. Well, we should be used to that. We accept so many conditions just to get by from day to day. For a promise as big as Love's promise, shouldn't we at least think about it a little? "Love one *another*," he said. Not "*Take* love from each other" but "*Love* one another." And that is all. That's the condition. Not that you live *for* love, but that you live *by* love's command. Not that you only *demand* love, but that you *give* it, from the endless store that, like some magic spring of sweet water, increases as it is given away, and only dries up if it is not used. Once you are fooled or frightened into seeking only your own satisfaction, you become isolated, alone. Your own ego becomes the cross on which you are nailed and then abandoned to suffer piteously and to no avail.

What Jesus promised was that, if we die to our own egos rather than on them, if we do this for *him*, and for the love he has guaranteed, and no matter what the other fellow does, then our joy would be complete.

He didn't promise that would always be easy to do. He didn't promise that love would not be betrayed again and again. But when that happens, he does not expect us to do anything he did not do. For Love's sake. Jesus, the guarantor of love for each one of us, was betrayed by one of his own, and then he was humiliated and tortured and hung on a cross. It wasn't what he wanted as a man. "Let this cup pass," he asked. But he gave his consent: "Not my will, but thine be done," he said. For love of each of us. And, as he hung there, blood clotted on his wounds and seeping into his lungs, he turned to the man who will always and gloriously be called "the disciple whom Jesus loved," and he gave his mother to him. And to us. He sealed us as his own. And then he died, for love of us.

The fact is: Everything he did then, he does continually. It wasn't wishful thinking on his part, nor mere metaphor. It was and is real. Then. Now. For all time. Forever. And, because he did all that he did, because he guaranteed *Love* in life and right through death itself, all the love we demand and all the love we give has its origin and its fulfillment in that *Love*. *That* is the magic spring of water! And, apart from it, there is no relief for our parched souls. Apart from it, there are pals and buddies, but no friends. Apart from it, there are parents and children, but no families. Apart from it, there is sex, with or without marriage, but there is no coming together in the oneness that may be the closest mirror of God's oneness that we can attain on earth. Apart from it, there are men and women who pay taxes and fight wars and hold down jobs, but no citizens and no patriots and no homeland. Apart from it, there is no meaning. And there is no love. In every age, in every life, in every circumstance, there is only one open question. And it isn't "Is there *still* love?" It is "What is *your* answer to Love?"

Still, just suppose, even knowing all that, that it's just too much to ask. This is a worldly time, and who's to say we shouldn't make our own conditions? Haven't people *always* said, "But *I* want to *be* loved!"

Yes. People have always said that. But they have said it only because God has said it first! And they can only demand it because he loved them first. Before they, before we, before anyone knew there was love, he loved us. And then he said, "Love me."

Since that late-evening conversation with my friend, every time I've heard her question, in whatever form, for whatever reason it's asked, I have wished with all my heart that, through some magic of time and space, I could take by the hand each one who asks, "Is there still love?" I have wished I could bring each of them to sit for a while by the side of one of those special people, one of those men and women who actually walked with God on his good earth and who learned to love from the heart of Love Itself. Perhaps if that woman I know (I've said to myself) could speak, say, with Mary Magdalene for just an hour; or if a young student I met not long ago could hear John the Apostle talk of the man he called Lord; or if a couple I have loved for these past eighteen years and who are now divorcing, could have talked to the bridal couple at Cana— maybe each of them, maybe each of us who wants to, would learn to say the words that the ever worldly, ever cynical Oscar Wilde did, words that might have come from the pen of a saint. The fact, he said, that Jesus loves us shows that "in the divine order, eternal love is to be given to what is eternally unworthy. Love is a sacrament that should be taken kneeling. And *Lord! I am not worthy* should be on the lips and in the heart of those who receive it."

❄

It is one of the mysteries of Jesus' love that his words and actions as a mortal man eternally fit the varying situations that arise in each age and in each individual life, fit in with all our lives.

By contrast, it is one of the greatest illusions cast over the person of Jesus today that he is likened to the "greats" of human history, that he is talked about as another one of those men and women who lived once upon a time, in a land far away or near, and whose images hang on the long walls of history's hall of fame.

It is true that the influence of such men and women is felt by others whom they never knew. But, to speak accurately about them, it is not they who now influence us, but what they left after them. Shakespeare. Newton. Alexander. Caesar. Add as many names as you care to, the list is small and definite. But when that list is done, there is no place in it for the name of Jesus of Nazareth.

For, of Jesus and of Jesus only is one thing true: though only a relatively small number of people ever saw him or heard him, still in whatever he did Jesus had before him, through the intimate knowledge he possessed as God, every individual woman, man, and child who did or would ever exist in the whole history of the universe, and each individual circumstance in which any one of them would find themselves. For, in whatever he did and said, Jesus did it and said it as God.

When he spoke to the blind man at Jericho who was cured because he believed. When he told the Rich Young Man the way to perfection. When he cleansed Mary Magdalene of her sins as she knelt before him and washed his feet with her tears—the mirror of every man and woman who has sought real love, sometimes in the wrong place, but ultimately with the loveliest of intentions. When he raised Lazarus from the dead. When he was with his eleven apostles for that last, loving meal the night before he died, and John the beloved disciple rested on Jesus' shoulder. At all those moments and in all of his time on earth, and in all of forever, present to Jesus' consciousness were and are all the past, all the foregone and accomplished yesterdays, as well as all the future, all the as-yet-to-come and as yet unlived tomorrows. His love, and all he said and did in that love, are exactly coextensive with each passing phase and mood of our individual lives.

Some people are not able to realize this powerful grasp Jesus has on all time and on all that happens to us in time, because they are confused about who Jesus was, is, and will always be. They think and speak about Jesus as if there were two different kinds of Jesuses. One is Jesus of Nazareth, the son of Mary, who was born in Bethlehem, lived a good and loyal and obedient life, was,—perhaps—the most moral man who ever lived; and who died and rose again from the tomb by the separate power of a distant God. The other is the Jesus who somehow or other "became" the son of God, had sonship "conferred" on him by the Father; was "elevated"—as a sort of brass ring, the grand prize for goodness—from being a mere human to being God's special and beloved son.

To think like that is to repeat a very old and deadening mistake. There is only one Jesus, one person who was and is God; who was, by his own will and with Mary's consent, conceived in the Virgin's womb; who was, by his own will, born as an infant; who grew up, preached, worked miracles, and, by his own will and consent, suffered, died a human death; and who, by his own power, rose again, his human body transfigured unchangeably by his own divine immortality and glory. "Jesus" is God's human name: "Who sees me, sees the Father . . . I and the Father are one."

Those who separate Jesus into two persons rob me of the love I must have, of the friendship that is my only hope, of the grace and holiness I need for the daily miracle of getting through my work, my difficulties, and for preserving my hopes and joy intact. His company is my only safeguard against the lovelessness that threatens all of us.

Because God was Mary's son; because God did live in a human body; because he walked as I walk, slept as I sleep, pained as I do; because he too loved and had special friends; because he died as I must, because he rose from death as I desire to rise; because God did all that as Jesus, Jesus as God—I have grounds for my hopes to surmount my weakness and to live forever. For I am only mortal flesh, after all. God in his love bridged the otherwise unbridgeable gap between my nothingness and his total being. And, because he did that, I know that he can bear with my weakness. I know that he can be melted by my fears. I know that he desires my love, wants my friendship.

That is why God became truly human: So that I, and

all of us, could be truly human and share his glory. For this, my savior was and is and will always be my God.

This then is the supreme advantage of Jesus as my savior and my friend and my ultimate recourse in all things. And it is in the realization of that advantage that Christians have always looked for ways to draw close to Jesus, and have always known that he would respond. It has been a kind of strategy of the faithful, one that enables us to live and to deal with the world around us, and to see in all of it the modern counterparts of the Gospel lessons. We can see Jesus' earthly life as a living backdrop of grace, love, and light available to us in our own daily lives.

That strategy seems very foreign to our world today. It is too harsh and realistic a time. Who can be so encased in the hard surface of impersonal mechanization, and still bend his knees and bow his head in prayer? Whose heart can be so filled with data and facts and formulas and actuarial tables, and still have room for love? Who can live this chapter in the history of our land, where it is increasingly the opinion that what is Christian is alien to what is American, and still have the heart to believe those few chapters in the human saga that tell of Jesus?

Who can do all of that? Anyone who, like some of the men and women of "Bible days," has the ears to hear and the eyes to see and the grace to believe. And so, as my taxicab driver said to me, I could tell you stories! Stories that may not at first seem to be love stories. And, yet, each one of them is a story in which love's offer is constantly made.

I have chosen five such stories from an endless number I could tell. Each of them is true, to a point. Each of them arrives at what seems an ending, a point at which there seems no more to say in a loveless world. But each such ending here is taken as another beginning, as an invitation to gather everything that has led to one bleak and loveless moment, and to hold all of it up to love's light, to play it out on the same stage, but in settings refurbished in the intimacy and contrast of Jesus' offer.

In each story, problems have caught up with someone at a time when he or she has been persuaded to forget or discount all we have heard about Jesus and about love. And in each story, there is portrayed some basic attitude toward love that is so common around us that anyone might simply sigh and say, "A pity, but that's the way of the world."

Who hasn't used love as a means to other ends, after all? Who hasn't seen "perfect marriages" crash into ruin? What youngster hasn't followed the siren song of "Why not?" Who hasn't seen love betrayed, or expected a return on every bit of love given?

With every invitation, it is up to the person who receives it to say yes or no. Love's invitation is no different. I don't know in fact whether all of the stories I've told here have ended as love stories. It will be clear that Laura M. did not find Mary Magdalene browsing one evening in her living room. But it will also be clear that, in one sense, she could have. The invitation is really there. Enough is known of Mary for her to be a backlighting for our lives at times, for us to think about her in such intimate terms that we do truly welcome her into our lives. And it is in just such ways—likely or unlikely—that people have always drawn close to Jesus. Such devices are the tools of love's strategy.

Not every love story can be told in one book, however

long that book might be. Not every invitation can be issued, and not every strategy of love at our disposal can be shown. I have tried to make up for that, at least in part, in the final chapter of this book. There I've sketched in broader terms some hint of the unending offer and the unchanging vision Jesus supplies, side by side with another offer and another vision that, in our time, would spread its mantle over us and transform our world.

In these pages, then, it is my prayer that many who want to, will, "kneeling and unworthy," stay for a time in the open and always flowering fields of faith, with some of those men and women who lived in the very company of Jesus, who heard his truth, saw his beauty, were strengthened with his strength, were comforted with his delicate understanding, learned to love with his love, and hoped for and found all that he promised.

For, say what you like, the "Bible days" have not ended. And they never will. And, say what you like, there is still love. And there always will be.

Chances and Changes

LOVE AS A MEANS TO AN END

Looking at Laura M., you would imagine that, if she wanted a taxi, for instance, even in the rain, one would appear by magic and whisk her away, dry and comfortable, through puddled streets, splashing rain on the more ordinary people who slogged toward home as best they could. Or that, if she felt hungry, it would always be in front of the most perfect little restaurant.

Not that Laura was beautiful. Her face was well proportioned, though, and expert makeup did the rest. Her figure was good. Elegant clothes made it even better. Conspicuous elegance—that was the mark of Laura M., the quality most of her more casual acquaintances remember about her.

There have always been women like Laura, and big cities have always been magnets for them. Big cities are impersonal, and whatever your ambition, you can, if you choose, do a lot of things to tilt the odds in your favor, things you might not so readily do "back home."

And what was Laura M.'s ambition? Have you ever

17

met the kind of person about whom everybody says, "I'd like to be like that"? That was the kind of person Laura wanted to be. That's what she wanted people to say when they looked at her. And when it seemed pretty clear that wasn't going to be the way of things for her in Davenport, Iowa, she simply left. She was, after all, twenty-three, and just how long should she be expected to wait? And wait for what? Most of the people she knew had "fallen in love," they said, and were married and lived in boring houses and worked and came home and worked and came home and . . .

That wasn't love; and, if it was, why it just didn't *lead* anywhere. "Change is the most interesting thing about people," she would say now and again. "With change there is always a chance . . ."

Laura didn't care which city she chose; the idea was to get there, get her bearings, learn where the "right" neighborhood was, head in that direction, and choose her stepping-stones, her chances and her changes, well.

Her first stepping-stone was easy to find, a retail modeling job in a very exclusive boutique, the kind where couples sit in chairs and "watch the girls go by," as the joke was among the models, in expensive clothes. That led quickly to the second stepping-stone.

He was married, but aside from that, perfect. Well, almost perfect. Love would have been nice, or at least marriage. To belong for sure where she thought it would be nice to be. But, still, he was wealthy, successful, discreet, not over-demanding on the one hand, and, on the other hand, really very generous. And, if he didn't "belong" to her for sure—and she to him—well at least she was as free as he was. All in all, it probably wasn't more than two or three months before Laura M. felt she could both quit her job and leave the apartment she had been sharing with a friend. She was on her way.

There are exceptions to every rule, and the exceptions to the "impersonal" rule of big city life are doormen, surely. George, the doorman at Laura M.'s new apartment building, was like a modern-day town crier. He knew a lot about everyone in his building, and he loved nothing better than a bit of good conversation.

"Used to be a model," George would confide to the man from the tenth floor or to the couple from the fifteenth or to whoever happened along as Laura M. passed through the door to the street. "You should see her apartment. She really did it up fine. Collections and all, and deep rugs, and classy furniture. I mean, good stuff. And those cupids and things on the wallpaper." George would wink to make sure you got the point. "Charlie the handyman put up some cabinets for her, and he says . . ." And so it went. Before long, Laura M. became a minor celebrity, at least among the tenants George knew. "Must be ten different men come to call in a week. Nice-looking chaps. Wonder how she keeps 'em all straight in her mind. You'd think she'd get mixed up."

Those in the building who got to know Laura M. a bit better than George did, those who had seen her apartment and been to a party or two there, knew he was right. The windows were elegantly draped. The carpets were deep, the furniture was luxurious. The sumptuous four-poster in her bedroom was canopied, and the room was done in delicate pastels. There was a very expensive stereo system and a large collection of tapes and records, many of them collector's items from the thirties and forties. But everything there was in perfect good taste. And it was beautiful in the bargain.

About all George got wrong was the part about "the cupids and things" on the wallpaper. There were none. Rather, there were well-executed paintings of nudes by San Gallo, and a fairly valuable collection of statuettes—history's better-known goddesses of love—a Venus, an Aphrodite, some Indian and African versions, and so on. Nothing vulgar—or, at least, not cheap-vulgar. It was all marked by the elegance that was Laura M.'s special trademark.

As with her apartment, her whole life was geared to her main interest. She dressed for morning and evening, according to the standards of the people who were "where she wanted to be." Her clothes were always conservatively elegant. She wore very little jewelry, and her makeup was so expert as to be practically undetectable.

The parties she gave were discreet and very enjoyable. And someone, a man, always stayed after the rest were gone. Not that Laura's life was all discreet parties at home. She went out as much as she stayed in, and to better and better places as the months went by. Sometimes, it was with a younger gentleman. Sometimes it was with one of the men she called her "lonely oldies." Sometimes they wanted a dinner companion, a theater companion, a traveling companion. Within a few years, in fact, Laura M. had seen a good part of the world. And always, whatever she did and whoever her companion was, it was sure to turn heads.

"I'd like to be like that," she would imagine strangers

saying to each other. Her dream come true! Elegance. Security. Luxury. The envy of others.

And there was love, too, make no mistake. Her men did love her. Or some did. All said they did. One left his wife on her account. There was even a rumor Laura had married secretly. But that wasn't true. She wasn't even tempted . . . except, perhaps, once. What could one man offer her that she didn't already have many times over— and without the boring sameness or the loss of freedom she had always claimed to detect in those who had gotten married? No, this was the best of all worlds, all in one. All in hers.

What probably came as a surprise to Laura—though it took a little time, of course—was that her world always seemed a step or two behind her dream. She kept trying to catch up. And, for all her easy elegance, she began to feel like a racer who couldn't find the finish line. It seemed, in fact, that her race was turning into a marathon, and that she would never get the prize. She wasn't sure after a time if she even knew what the prize was supposed to be.

Her building became a condominium, and she bought her own apartment and one more in the building. She bought a new painting, had her bedroom repapered and the bathroom redone, and had a prominent interior designer decorate the new annex to her apartment. She was seen at the right places for weekends; the fashionable restaurants for dinner; the right hotels in London, Rio, Rome, Hong Kong. Always calm and at her ease. Always dressed just right, whatever the occasion. Always with elegant, rich men. She even had some amount of real influence after a while, and a certain not-quite-tarnished social standing. After all, she knew a remarkable number of the right men. Didn't George always wonder how she kept her calendar straight? He meant her men. Oh, she knew about George and his busy tongue!

The thing was, she had always thought that would be *it*. Surely in all of that, she should have found the prize. Or at least *a* prize. Or at least *part* of a prize.

"Funny thing," George began to say to this or that tenant as he let the street door close behind Laura M., "All that money and all those things and friends, and she makes me feel kind of sad."

I don't know if Laura knew that George said that. And I don't know if George knew how close to the bone he came with that remark. But it was true that people saw genuine happiness on her face only on a few typical occasions. On early mornings with fresh sunlight and brisk weather brightening up the streets, she looked girlish and spontaneously joyful as she walked in blue jeans and a sweater. Or doing household errands out amid the bustle of the city. Or pushing her cartful of groceries in the cash register line at the supermarket, you saw happiness in her walk, her greeting, her easy way of treating people. She was relaxed, casual, nonchalant, almost jaunty, certainly charming in a conversational way.

Apart from such occasions, Laura M. wore what George used to call her "look." It was meant to be attractive in a worldly way—and it was. She affected a certain air of expectancy that reminded you of a schoolgirl on the eve of a great vacation. But at the same time, there was a subtle smugness about it, traces of some secret exultancy, as if that look said, "I am here to be seen, marveled at, desired, envied, because I am a mystery and I have power, and I am not drudging at a daily grind like a lot of others."

What that look meant was that Laura was viewing all the things and all the people around her from the world of her private dreams, her very personal aims. Everything else left her cold and unresponsive. The "look" was a contrived thing. It was the most obvious sign of the real prostitution Laura M. practiced. Something as sacred as innocence was being harnessed to something else that was quite un-innocent.

Only rarely, a quick glance might catch Laura off her guard and detect traces of some marked sadness.

Laura's mother came to visit her from Davenport once and things did seem to brighten up a bit. Laura was really happy to see Mrs. M. and to hear all the news from home. But it didn't last long.

"Of course, I didn't say anything," George shook his head. "But Mrs. M. was no dope. She figured out how her daughter manages to live like that, no regular job and all."

Mrs. M. wasn't angry exactly. Children are very independent nowadays. What mother didn't learn *that*, she sighed to herself. Why, she knew many cases right at home in Davenport! And hadn't Laura always been more independent than most? And, after all, she wasn't a child anymore. Not anymore.

But Mrs. M. was sad. For herself. And for Laura, too. What she felt, in fact, was Love's own sadness, and it was very hard for her to hide that sadness altogether. Whatever about strangers, here was one woman, the closest person Laura M. had, the one person who always would say unfailingly, "I love you," but who would never say, "I'd like to be like you."

A month or two after Mrs. M. went back to Davenport,

Laura left, too, for what looked like a long trip. George heaped her suitcases into the trunk of a long limousine. He didn't get a good look at the man inside. George tried to find out where they were going. That was George's way. But the chauffeur either didn't know or wasn't saying.

"Mind things for me, George," Laura smiled and gave him a big tip and one of the several keys to her apartment she always kept handy.

"Yes, ma'am," George said. No mistake: she looked sad.

That was a few months ago, and Laura M. hasn't come back yet. George misses her. But, then, as I said, doormen are the exceptions to the rule.

❄

The most striking thing about Laura M., it always seemed to me, wasn't the elegance that Laura and so many of her acquaintances thought of as her trademark. It was her sameness. It seems to me that I have seen Lauras all my life, wherever I've traveled. And I think that there have been Lauras by the thousands, everywhere and in every generation. Not all of them are as striking as Laura. Not all of them are as appealing, for Laura is appealing in her way. Not all of them misunderstand in exactly the way Laura did. And not all of them by any means are women. For the fact is that now, with all the restraints off, more people seem to say, as Laura wanted them to, "I'd like to be like that."

Still, restraints or not, elegant or not, sooner or later, something seems to show in the eyes of people who make that choice and then follow the tide it sets up in their lives. George saw it in Laura and he called it sadness. But I think it is the look of love's promise misunderstood. For many, it becomes love's promise lost.

The misunderstanding of love's promise concerns our willingness to see love as an instrument for our use, rather than as a basic condition of life. It concerns mistaking love for the mere means love uses to bind us to itself. Love is cheapened by that mistake to something almost tangible— often, to something merely physical. It is taken as something we can use for barter, in exchange perhaps for delight, for comfort, for pleasure, for satisfaction, to stave off loneliness. For a thousand other things.

We thus renege on love, quite simply: by *using* love. That is the only way we can renege on love—by using it for profit, for jealousy, for getting even, for mere enjoyment, for survival. In a word, as a means for sheer self-interest. But Jesus taught that love cannot be a means of livelihood, or a means of persuasion, or a means to gain power, or any other sort of means or tool to be used for other goals. Love *is* persuasion. Love *is* power of a gentle, strong sort. Love *is* the goal. You don't choose to reach some target with love. You choose other things, anything that comes up for consideration in your life, in order to reach love.

But if we make that mistake of using love as a means or tool, when we mistake the means and signs and benefits of love for love itself, then we transform love's most sacred expressions into tariff-takers. And we transform the spaciousness of our innermost selves, where our desire and need for love reside, into a sort of counting house where we deposit the coins of benefit and pleasure. Harsh as it may sound, we prostitute love.

Our sadness grows because love is the one thing about

us that is not an instrument for, or subservient to, anything else. And it cannot be replaced by any substitute. A hand, an arm, a leg is an instrument for our use. If need be, we can get along without an organ or a limb, though we would rather not have to. Even hearts and kidneys can sometimes be transplanted. But there is no substitute for love. Nothing can be transplanted to replace love's most vital, most basic work in our mortal selves.

Like everything about us, that innermost "space" within us that we so often try to fill with life's coinage has been fashioned by Love's own hand, as Love's own dwelling. That "space" is our capacity to receive Love itself and then to mirror it in our very selves, and in our lives. Not to *use* it, but to *mirror* it—minute by minute, day by day, decade by decade—in all we are and in all we do.

That seems a lot to ask in a time when substitutes for love are held out not merely as normal and right, but as life's most wonderful offerings to us. The curious thing is that so many of us seem confused when those wonderful prizes of life desert us; or when, even if the prizes are plentiful, they never seem to fill that space where Love should dwell. Often, even as we are counting those wonderful prizes of life that we have acquired, we feel sad and emptied out, as though someone has stolen into our private counting house and cheated us of our treasure. And often that is exactly what has happened.

We all understand that sadness. We all have felt it whenever we have sold one pearl of love's treasure for something—anything—less than love itself.

Thinking of Laura—and of others who are a little like her in ways—has made me wish I could take her by the hand and introduce her to one very special woman whom I have grown to love. What a moment that would be! From all we know about her in the Gospels and in long and hallowed Christian tradition, she spent some years on that same marathon that attracted Laura. I've imagined that meeting in detail, and I can tell you: that would be a moment, if ever it could take place . . .

❋

"Who's there?" Laura called out from her bedroom when she heard the front door click shut. She wasn't frightened. George was a careful doorman, and she knew several people had keys. But she wasn't expecting anyone just now—she was sure of that. She managed her schedule very well. She had to.

"Who's there?" she called again. Annoyed when there was no answer, she strode through the door to the living room, her Balmain dressing gown flowing with that elegance she liked so. To her amazement, there was a woman, a total stranger already quite at home there, browsing about among the statuettes and paintings and records.

Laura's first thought was that this was some man's irate wife come to make a scene. Who could have been so careless? She tried to think of some disarming thing to say, some way to catch this Mrs. Whoever off balance before a scene could begin. But all that came out was a very ordinary "Who are you? Where did you come from? How did you get in here?" The words tumbled out like one single question.

Her visitor turned what seemed a very lovely face to Laura for the first time, and smiled as she took a long, studied look. She didn't *seem* irate. But a woman in Laura's position couldn't be too careful.

"I am called Mary," Mrs. Whoever answered each of Laura's tumbled-out questions directly. "I came, in the sense you mean, from Magdala. And I got in with this key." She held her hand out and Laura snatched the key from her palm. "There seem to be quite a number of them," Mary smiled again, as she withdrew her empty palm.

"Mary?" Laura repeated, giving herself time to go over the first names of the wives of her gentlemen, about whom she knew almost everything. Everything needful, at least. Her mind came up a blank. "Your last name, Mrs.—er—." She was trying to be natural. And she tried to get some clue from the way this intruder, this Mrs. Mary, was dressed. She'd always found there was a look about the wives of her gentlemen. Lawyers' wives. Corporate wives. Wives of chairmen of boards. They all had a kind of uniform, as Laura called it. Not elegant. Not really. But this woman smashed that mold. Laura had never seen anything quite like this.

"Do you like it, Laura?" Mary noticed Laura's lingering look at the linen gown she was wearing. "It's the finest sheer linen. *Byssos* linen, it's called. From Tyre. You can draw the whole thing through the ring on your finger. Imagine! And it won't even be wrinkled! Here, feel it!"

Laura was tempted, almost reached out her hand. But it might be a trap. She was the one being caught off guard. She'd have none of that! "Do you have a last name, by any chance?" Laura repeated her question almost insultingly.

"Of course," Mary settled comfortably into the deep cushioned sofa. "But it wouldn't mean anything to you. Matthew—he was the first to write about what happened, you know—Matthew called me Mary Magdalene. And that's how everyone knows me." She beamed at Laura.

"Mary Magdal—. Matthew—." Laura's knees went weak. She sat down. Oddly enough, she didn't think this was some charade, some joke being played on her. Somehow, she knew. And that was strange, because Laura was not religious. She knew people who went to church—among them, some of her gentlemen. But for Laura, once out of Davenport, religion was strictly live-and-let-live.

"You look a little pale, Laura." Mary's concern was genuine. "Can I get you some water?"

Laura shook her head. She didn't want water. Understandably, she was unable to speak: she believed the unbelievable. And so, Mary knew, that was step one. Who would know better than Mary of Magdala the difficulty of that first step?

"Your home is elegantly done." From anyone else but the Magdalene, this might have been a polite way of filling the silence till her hostess could regain her composure. In a sense, it *was* an easeful way to begin step two. Mary reached her hand out and picked up a statuette of Astarte, the old Hebrew goddess of love, from the collection on the table nearest them. "I had one just like that. I wouldn't be surprised if it was the very same. This looks very old. And valuable."

"Yes, a friend . . ." Laura's voice was a little breathy, but she was coming around. She'd be fine in a minute or two.

"In fact, Laura—you won't believe this—much of what you have here, allowing for the changes over two thousand years and thousands of miles, is what I might have had at home in my native Magdala.

"Even this city! After all, in its day, Magdala was a

major center of trade for all the surrounding countries. All of them, north and south and east, came to us with their silks and perfumes. Of all the nine cities that ringed the shores of Lake Galilee, none attracted richer caravans than Magdala.

"So it wasn't hard for me to come by the best. Just as you have, in this magnificent city. We even had a stock exchange of a kind. And theaters and games and parties." She waved a hand and the gesture seemed to include the entire room where they sat for all the world like two old friends just catching up, Mary telling Laura about the life she had lived two thousand years before this day.

It all sounded to Laura remarkably like her own life. After the first shock, perhaps it was that sameness that fascinated her so. Hadn't her mother always said, the more things change, the more they remain the same?

She was fascinated as Mary told about her travels to Egypt and Syria and Sidon and Tyre and Beirut and Damascus. Laura had been to several of those places and, as Mary described them now, they didn't sound all that different from the way Laura found them. The hills and the river gullies dried up in the summer sun, and the desert and the olive trees and such. Sometimes Mary had traveled with a companion, as Laura had. Sometimes she would go alone on what she described as a well-deserved buying spree.

At home in Magdala, Mary said, she had lived in her own house on a very fashionable street.

"Laura," the unusual visitor chatted on easily, weaving Laura into the fabric of her life for a reason she wasn't ready to disclose yet. "If you could have seen my house, I know you would have wanted everything there. There were little statues of your friends." She nodded toward the statues of Cupid and Venus around the room. "That sort of thing provided a suitable atmosphere for my visitors. And that seemed only right. After all, it was the visitors who helped make it all possible!"

Everyone in her Magdala neighborhood knew Mary, but there had been no raised eyebrows. "Big cities are uncomplicated that way," Mary observed thoughtfully.

Laura nodded. She knew.

Of course, Mary didn't participate in any of the religious celebrations of Judaism. But in a large city like Magdala there were so many like her, it made no practical difference in her life. As to the rest, she had what everyone had—only, more of it. And there was no one she had to answer to, as most of the women of her time did.

Mary had her problems, of course, like everyone else. But she would talk them over with this friend or that, or somehow find the help she needed. There was no question of her going to the local rabbi or to one of the elders of the Magdala Synagogue or to one of the wise Pharisees. For people of Mary's acquaintance, such men were fair game for hilarious jokes and were considered to be backward-minded spoilsports.

There were very ancient accounts about her, as Mary knew, accounts of her having been married once, and of war and death. But Mary waved all that aside in her mind. She hadn't come to see this beloved Laura to settle the arguments of Bible scholars. Faith, she knew, had other needs. Who would know better than the Magdalene?

But she did tell Laura with disarming frankness how she used to think about love. It was a kind of power for her, she said, but a power that carried no responsibility for her, except to her own happiness and her own success.

"Men were useful," Mary said, "like—."

"Like stepping-stones?" Laura knew very well every bit of the life and thinking Mary was describing. The more things change. . . .

"Yes." Mary smiled a soft smile. (Her face really was lovely, Laura thought. Not beautiful. But lovely.) "I thought perhaps somewhere along the way I would find love. And I told myself that if anyone was in a position to find it, I was. But somehow it all turned into the business of pleasure; and then there wasn't much pleasure; and then there wasn't much point in even thinking about love anymore. I didn't really know what had happened—or that anything had changed. It was as though something in me had gone blank or empty, but I hadn't got the full impact yet. Like having a little ache and a sniffle before the full fever sets in."

Laura thought that sounded familiar, too. In fact, she thought she was past the sniffles and going into high fever! She glanced toward the shelves that held her record collection, a little musical memory playing bitterly at the edges of her mind. The Mills Brothers, was it? Yes. A valuable first edition. Oh, yes. "You're Nobody Till Somebody Loves You," she said the title half aloud. Then, for Mary's benefit: "A song they sang years ago. A 'golden oldie' they call it now. A gift from a—er—a friend." A gift, in fact, from one of Laura's "lonely oldies." Appropriate for him as well as for her, she thought: "You're Nobody Till . . ."

"Well," Mary's voice cut off the self-pity that tempted Laura's mind away from the story. "One day I felt a little the way you do now." That lovely smile of hers again, like balm to Laura. There seemed no self-interest in this woman.

It was beginning to dawn on Laura, in fact, that Mary Magdalene had come bearing gifts freely. And this story was the gift. Mary's prize. She listened with full attention now.

"That day," Mary went on, "I expected no visitors, nothing to help cheer me up. So I decided to go out, perhaps to buy a little something to lift my spirits. The streets of Magdala were always busy with caravans and businessmen, and the usual shouting and clatter. You know how it is. So, when I heard some loud cries and a woman's screams and pleading over all the din, it caught my attention, you can be sure.

"Just a little distance ahead of me I saw it, then. It was an ugly scene. I had seen the animal in men often before, but this was different. A whole group of them, faces distorted with anger and hate, obscenities pouring out of their mouths. 'Whore!' one of them shouted above the rest. And then, like a chant, the word was taken up by all of them. 'Whore! Whore! Whore!'

"It was ugly and hateful and mesmerizing. I clamped my hands over my ears. The pain of it was almost physical for me. But I was riveted there.

"Then I saw her. Just as the first screaming brute picked up a stone, I saw her. She was cringing, crouching on the ground, already bleeding from the head and shoulders. 'My God! There is blood upon her,' I said to myself. 'Oh, God! Oh God!' It was the closest thing to a prayer I'd said in twenty years. And I just kept saying it again and again. 'Oh God! Oh God! I don't want to see this. Oh God!'

"I couldn't stand it. But I couldn't leave either. I closed my eyes tightly. Then, with no warning, very suddenly, everything was quiet. 'They've killed her!' I thought. 'I can't look. They've killed her.'

"I opened my eyes expecting to see real carnage. But instead, it was like a tableau. Everyone was frozen, arms raised, stones in hands, mouths open, but as though frozen. No one spoke. No one moved.

"And then I saw him. He walked out from a group of men, fishermen and laborers mostly, by the look of them. But he was different. Not just different from his companions. But different from everyone there. All eyes there were upon him. I wasn't sure if he had spoken. But something he said or something he did or something about him had suddenly stopped that hideous chant. Maybe it was that quiet strength. It wasn't overbearing, but it was immediate and, it seemed to me, irresistible. Or maybe it was his gentleness, so powerful that it was like a hand hushing the hate, seeming of itself somehow to quiet the killing noise.

"He was beautiful. Oh, not just in the way I had always thought of men as beautiful. It wasn't that. It was real. Sensual, some might think, but not sexual. It bypassed sexuality, but it produced in me a feeling of peace and sweetness that sex—at least the kind of sex I had known, the kind that poor woman crouching there had known—only leaves a yearning for.

"He walked right into that maddened crowd. Easily. And they parted for him. He walked near to where that woman still cringed. Then he turned to face the men, their hands still holding stones, raised and threatening. He seemed to look into every face there, but it took no time at all. And he asked a single question: 'Why?'

"They were quick to answer: 'We caught her in adultery. The Law says she must die by stoning.'

"I was breathless. I couldn't imagine he could hold them back for long. But then he did the most startling thing. As though there were no danger at all, he squatted down near the woman, picked up a stick, and began scratching something in the dust of the street. Just like that, as though he had all the time and all the authority in the world.

"I suppose everyone else was startled, too. And curious. One man leaned a little closer to see what words the stick was tracing there. Then another man bent over. And another. I heard later that they saw their own names scratched clearly in the dust, one by one. And the names of women, not their wives, they had been with. But it wasn't a threat to tell the world. He made that clear in the next instant.

"When he spoke finally, his voice was just like his appearance. It was strength itself. And gentleness. And authority. 'Let the first stone come from the hand of the man who has not sinned,' he said.

"There was a buzz of consternation among the threatening men. For the first time I looked around at them more carefully. I knew them, or some of them, anyway. And they had known me or one of my friends. Perhaps my name was even scratched in that patch of street dust! First one, then three, then ten or eleven of them let the stones drop from their hands to the ground, and turned their backs on the woman.

"When there were none of them left, and without even rising to his feet, this wonderful intruder into disaster spoke to the woman for the first time. 'Where are your accusers?' That special voice again, and that sweetness inside me when I heard it. She didn't answer him. She just looked at him, still dazed.

"He spoke again: 'Has no one condemned you?'

"She was able to answer by then, but barely: 'No one.'

"Then, he stood up and took her by the hand to help her to her feet. And I could hardly believe what I saw on that face of hers. With all the stains of blood and tears and dirt, I saw a radiance I had never seen on another human face. Not just relief. Not just fear banished. I hadn't seen it since I was the tiniest child, but I knew it as well as if I had seen it all my life. I saw love. And I saw belovedness. That woman knew at that moment, despite all the hate that had held her to the ground before my very eyes, and despite her own lacks and needs and betrayals, despite everything, she knew she was loved. It was as if a whole cleansing had passed between that man who faced her and the woman he beheld. As though her whole soul was before God and had been cleansed by the Spirit. 'Neither shall I condemn you,' he said to her. 'Go now. Sin no more.'

"I thought I saw the woman shiver just a little, the way children do at some great news or a special gift. Or maybe it was I who shivered. For everything he said to her, I felt he had said to me. When he looked at her face, I felt the look as surely as if I had been in her place and been helped to my feet by him. At one moment, it seemed to me, I, not that woman, had been cowering, hated and bloodied and dirty. The next moment, I was as alive, radiant and happy

—truly happy—and as truly at peace as that poor but oh so fortunate woman.

"She obeyed him then. She walked slowly away, looking back, but knowing, I'm sure, that she was not leaving behind what she had been given: a love that would not change or disappear or desert her. There was a beautiful happiness on her face."

Mary was silent for a while, and for Laura it was as though this now welcome intruder was sharing with her the same love Jesus had shared with that woman. For Laura knew the story. She knew Jesus was that man. She had read the Gospel. Not for years, but she had read it, the way she had read a thousand stories. Now, though, hearing it all from this woman who had heard those precious words from the mouth of Jesus himself, it was like being warmed with Mary in the same cloak, protected against a chilling wind. She didn't want to think about that chill. She didn't want to break the spell. So she said nothing. She waited. And, in time, Mary went on.

"When this man turned to leave, his companions joined him, and they passed near me. I stopped one of them—the youngest, he appeared to me. That was the first time I spoke to John or to any of that group. I asked him who that woman's remarkable savior was. And that was the first time I heard the name. The young man said, 'Jesus. Jesus from Nazareth.' I asked many more questions, not wanting to be parted from what seemed a new light, a sun, a brightness. He told me he didn't know how long they would be in Magdala, and that in the evening Jesus would be dining with the Rabbi Simon. He told me more, but those two things were all I remembered then, because

I only cared at that moment about that light, about not losing it, about getting closer to it, about getting to the man who brought it and shared it with others.

"I went back to my house. That was a strange experience, going back there. I had lived there for years, and had chosen everything in it myself. But it was like walking into a place for the first time. All my expensive furniture, my statuettes of the love goddess, my comfortable couches, all my decorations—all appeared dismal. And all the signs of love I had hung around the house seemed like so many terrible jokes, making fun of something they knew nothing about. But really all of that barely crossed my thoughts, like a tiny shadow.

"My attention, my mind, my whole being was focused on just one thing. In just a brief time that morning, I had found what my whole life had been about—or what I had thought it had been about. In that brief time, hate and blame and tawdry betrayal and certain death had been transformed before my very eyes into the complete opposite. Love. Forgiveness. Safety. I didn't want to lose any of that.

"For most of that day, I thought about all that had happened. 'Neither shall I condemn you.' I repeated the words Jesus had said to the woman, asking myself what kind of a man could say those words. 'Neither shall I condemn you. Go now. Sin no more.' Whatever he meant by those words, I had no idea then. It was surely something more than the authority with which he said them, and more than that gentleness. And that love. Yet, that was the total meaning of it all for me.

"By evening time, I knew everything was changed for me. I didn't bother about the details. It would be step-by-step. But I knew, suddenly, I knew the first step. I had to get to Jesus.

"You should have seen me! I raced about the house. I changed into this very gown. I took the best alabaster jar I had and filled it full of the most precious fragranced cream. I had plenty of that. How I had wasted it over the years! Then I fairly ran through the streets until I reached the door of the Rabbi's house.

"For a moment, I paused out there in the street. I could hear the talk and the laughter. Men's talk. Men's laughter. I brushed past the startled servants near the door. No women were allowed to eat with the men. And no woman with my reputation had ever passed through the Rabbi's door before, I promise you that!

"Inside the main court where the guests were dining I searched for him in the crowd of faces. I heard someone nearby whisper my name to his companion. And then another whisper, until the laughter and the talk had all become whispers, and all the faces turned toward me and the flush of the wine drained from at least half of them. They knew me, those suddenly pale-faced gentlemen!

"Out of the corner of my eye, I saw the Rabbi rise from his place and start toward me, anger clearly on his face. At the same time, I saw Jesus. I had missed him at first, because I thought he would be the guest of honor, seated next to Simon. But no. There he was, far across the courtyard, far from the more prominent guests, at a table that had not even been served, with young John and the others in his company.

"Before Simon had taken three steps toward me, I was across the courtyard, weeping with joy, kneeling at the feet of Jesus. I couldn't stop my tears. It was as if all the joy and all the pain and all that mattered ever to me were flowing freely at last in those tears. And they fell on his feet. I loosened my hair and dried them. And then I opened the alabaster jar. The aroma of the cream filled the courtyard. For the second time that day, no one moved. I rubbed the cream over the feet of Jesus.

"The whispering redoubled. I knew what they were saying. And Jesus certainly knew what they were saying, and what Rabbi Simon was saying. 'If this man were truly a prophet, he would not put up with this! Imagine, allowing himself to be touched by the hands of a public harlot!'

"Then, just as he had done that morning, with the same authority and that gentle strength, Jesus put an end to all the muttering. 'Simon,' Jesus' voice carried easily, 'I have something to say to you.'

" 'Yes, Master.' Simon could hardly control the derision in his voice.

" 'You object to this woman touching me. Her hands are the hands of a public sinner. Is that not so? Yet her hands are doing what yours did not, what yours should have done. You did not do for me what every host does for his guests. You did not refresh me with water for my feet. This woman washes my feet with her tears. You welcomed me with no embrace. But she covers my feet with her kisses. You welcomed me with no perfumed oil. But this woman anoints my feet with this fragranced cream.

" 'And so while you whisper with your honored guests against this woman and against me, I say, her sins, which are many, are forgiven. For she has loved much.' His eyes covered the courtyard with that glance of his. 'Little is forgiven to those who love little.' Finally, he turned his eyes

down toward me, just as he had toward that poor bloodied
woman in the street that morning. And he gave his hand
to me as he had to her. And he said to me as he had to her:
'Your sins are forgiven you.' "

For the second time, Mary lapsed into silence. Every
image Mary recalled in her story seemed present to Laura.
As if she herself had been there. As if the tears that came to
her own eyes now, had been the ones that wet the feet of
Jesus. As if her hand had been the one Jesus had reached
out for. As if—.

But no. Laura M., the practical woman around town,
asserted herself. No. This was now. This was another time.
Another century. Another world. Another life. She was
Laura M. Not Mary of Magdala.

Mary sensed the reversal of feeling, understood the
fight going on inside Laura M. For the first time since she
had sat down there, Mary rose from the armchair and
moved around the room, touching this and that object.
Laura followed her with her eyes, unbelieving. She saw the
room in which she had lived and entertained guests for
years now, as Mary had seen her own house that day when
she had met Jesus. All was changed.

Or was it?

"I see what you're saying," Laura M. finally said. "I see
what you are trying to do for me. And I'm grateful. Really,
I am. But it's different for me. You were with him. You
touched him. You really saw him and knew him and he
explained things to you."

"But now *you* have seen what he did. You *saw* it
through my eyes. You felt it *with* me!" So far, Mary of
Magdala had not spoken as fervently as this to Laura.
"And now that you have that much of it—of his love in

you, even that tiny bit of his love in you—isn't it enough to fill your whole world?"

Laura M. nodded. She said nothing, but she did at least nod. The beginning of "yes."

Mary came closer again. "I want to tell you, if you have that much of his love in you—and you have, we both know you have—it's not my doing. Believe me. It's Jesus. Jesus himself. That's his power. That's what makes him different from any other. Think a little. Doesn't something inside you tell you this: 'This is his doing. It is Jesus himself who has touched my soul'?"

The expressions on Laura M.'s face were totally open now. None of that "look." No disguises. The expressions changed from perplexed to angry to dismayed to hopeful. Mary watched these changes, trusting that a new realization of love was dawning on Laura. Yes! Laura's face told Mary: Yes, she was changing, just as she herself had changed at the first brush with Jesus. Perhaps, too, like the laborers in Jesus' own parable who came later in the day than the other workers, but who were paid as much as those who had started at the beginning of the day. And so sweetly changed. It must be—Jesus. His power. It must be!

And so, without complications or long explanations, but merely drinking in, sharing the passionate faith of this one loving woman, Laura perceived the fundamental element of our relationship with Jesus: His ever presence with each one of us, and his personal commitment to each one of us, individually.

For, our savior, Jesus, says to Laura, to me, to each other person, I am closer to you than your own body, than your thoughts. I know your body. I know your thoughts.

There is not one bone or one drop of your blood, any more than there is one moment of your consciousness, that is not present to me. I have known all about you from the time you were conceived. I was with you all the days and all the nights and all the years until this moment. And I shall always be that close to you. For one reason: I love you. I am Love itself. And I am your savior. *Your* personal savior. I have never had to accept you, because I have possessed you since your existence began. Will you not accept me as Love?

And Jesus says to Laura, to me, to each person: "You want to know what I think and feel about this action of yours, that undertaking of yours, those friends or those enemies of yours, that sickness of yours, that success of yours. Read the Gospel. Read the story of my life among men and women. And know that my life is not ended. Know that when I said, 'Remain in my love,' I knew you. When I said, 'Come follow me,' I was speaking to you. I did nothing, said nothing, suffered nothing, enjoyed nothing, achieved nothing, without having you in mind. For I love you."

All of that was what Laura M. began to understand simply, directly, for the first time. What she saw now, wordlessly but completely—the way she might have come upon a street she had never traveled—was something that never changed, was never the plaything of chance, was always there. She saw Love.

Mary knew she had understood. "Then, answer my question," the Magdalene said. "Now that you've seen it, can you possibly want to lose it? Would that not be like being bathed with the very light of love, and then saying, 'Put out that light!' Can you possibly give that away, now

that it's within your reach and grasp, give it away for—"
Mary glanced around the room again, raising her hands in
an all-inclusive gesture "—for this? For anything? Can
you?"

Everything depended on her answer; Laura saw that
clearly. All of her past. All of her future. All the time she
had left. And beyond. All depended on her answer. (Dear
God! Why must I answer that question now?) But there
was no way of avoiding it. Even if she chose to say nothing,
do nothing, that would be her answer. Even if she let this
woman depart in silence, without her answer, that would
be her answer.

There are brief moments in life when the pressure of
reality falls on us heavily, too heavily, and, we are sure, too
cruelly. No excuse will shield us from such a moment.
No putting it off will do. The thing is too real. We have to
decide. And at that moment, all our human loneliness and
weakness surfaces. Our desire not to "face it alone" is
sharpened. We feel the ache and the pain of taking a deci-
sive stand, of saying good-bye to what was once for us the
sweetness of existence, the spice of life, perhaps the only
thing we ever wanted. We are cornered, squeezed against
the wall. At such moments, the tears of helplessness well
unbidden to our eyes. We cannot share that moment with
anyone—except our sweet and loving savior, Jesus. Only he
understands it.

Yet, just such moments are precious in his eyes. Just
such moments are gifts from him, occasions of choice, of
his love offered and of our response. And, so, in such a
moment, all our weakling condition as creatures emerges,
naked and vulnerable. We seem for just that time to be
standing without shelter between a house we have known

and one we have never entered. We may even feel, as St. Paul felt on such an occasion, that the trial "is too great for our strength." At that moment we feel we need many things.

Jesus knows that what we do need then is compassion—supremely, compassion. He answers as he answered St. Paul. "My grace is sufficient for you."

Such a moment has come—once or many times—to every person who has been offered the hand of God. One Psalm of David's chants twenty-seven times, His compassion endures for ever! As if to remind us that his compassion is endless. And that compassion now touched Laura M. so that even those salt tears of hers were somehow a release, washing away her bondage to "chances and changes," opening up a tiny way for her, a different path, another choice. As the tears of Mary Magdalene that washed the feet of Jesus had done. "In the greatness of your compassion, wipe out my offense,"—another prayer of David's was in those tears.

Mary saw Laura's tears in the same way Jesus had seen hers. She spoke quickly, encouragingly, facing with Laura the difficulty of making the choice of Love. "Many others had to answer that same question." She gestured with a nod and a lift of the eyebrows. "Women and men. Boys and girls. Of every age. In every age. None of them were really different from you. Not in what really matters. I saw a very rich, very moral young bachelor"—she threw a glance at Laura M.—"you've come across that type, too, haven't you? Well, Jesus loved this man, invited him to stay, to join him. But the young man couldn't say good-bye to all that money and all that power and prestige. He wasn't a bad man. He always observed the Law. You must understand that. And he didn't say no. He only looked sad, and walked away.

"And there were scores of others—Roman centurions, Temple officers, tradesmen, divorced women, mothers with dying sons and daughters. There was Judas Iskariot —the cleverest of the lot!—and even King Herod, the most cultured man of his time. Love knocked at his door, too. I remember one whole flock of people who had faithfully followed Jesus everywhere, drinking in everything he said. One day he told them and everyone else, too, that in order to enter his kingdom they would have to eat his flesh and drink his blood. It was sad to see how they rejected this. They disputed. They grumbled and groused. They threatened to leave him. But Jesus kept on saying the same thing: "You must drink my blood and eat my flesh, in order to have a part in my kingdom." And many of them simply left him. And, Laura, he did not force them to stay. You see, it is always *his* offer. But it is always *our* choice. The choice of each person, each one.

"That day, the choice was to trust love. You see, those of us who did stay really didn't understand any more than the ones who left him. At least, we didn't understand with our heads. We did understand with our hearts, with our spirit, with something greater and more discerning than merely our minds. We trusted. And therefore we didn't lose love."

"Trust." Laura repeated that one word as though it were in a strange language. It had been a long time since she had really trusted anyone, or had asked for trust herself. Hadn't she lived by chances and by changes? Nevertheless, all the while Mary had been speaking, images had been gathering up in Laura's mind. Images of her life, her possessions, her travels, her friends, such as they were. All that seemed as worthless as cinders compared to what she was now offered.

"Does it mean that I have to be alone?" Laura was finally pinning down her greatest fear. All her life, even the threat of being alone frightened her. It was the last great hurdle in the way of her choosing Jesus and his love. And what was lacking to her was a measure of belief, a full realization of who Jesus is.

"When I speak of love, Laura, I am talking about a person. A real person. About Jesus." With those few reassuring words, Mary touched on the central need: belief in Jesus.

For the Jesus who is love, and whom we are asked to choose above all else, is a real person with mind and imagination and will and likes and dislikes and a manner that is unmistakably his own—a real person. Jesus is not just a man they tell you about in Sunday school, who died far away and thousands of years ago. Not just a saintly memory. Not just the long-dead-and-buried gentlest of heroes. He is alive. Living. Thinking. Willing. Working. Yesterday. Today. Tomorrow. Next year. For all our years. He is there. He always will be. For every bit of love we find in this mortal universe—Jesus is needed for it in the very condition required for love among us. Miss that point, and you likely miss love. Miss that point, and loneliness is sure to come. For only he is love. And, all over, we shall find traces and signs, sometimes floods, of his love.

Mary drove her lesson home to Laura simply: "If ever —I mean, *ever!*—you felt the slightest twinge of love, real love, for any of your men friends—just the tiniest little grip on your heart—then that was because of Jesus."

Yes, Laura immediately thought—there was that one time, that one man. He didn't want what all the others wanted. He said he loved her and wanted to marry her. Yes! What's that he had said? Something about her getting out of this prison of her life and seeing the wide world of God in his company, and as his wife.

At the moment, yes, she had felt the touch of love. Felt as if something grand and powerful had touched her. But how could she trust one man? Chance and change had been her only real partners. They had gotten her everything. Had she understood that offer to see the wide world of God in one man's company, the realization would have been so great, it could have been a blow to her brain. All the pretense, the false hopes, the arrogance she had entertained all those years with all those people, the never-ever expectation she had nourished—it would all have dropped away from her. But that first grand moment in her life had dropped away instead.

And, so, everything hung on this, a second moment, the final change, the ultimate chance to say yes to Love's offer, to discover that it is simple, easy, natural. The only extraordinary thing about it all seems to be our wonder, often, that we got along seemingly well without it at all; until we reflect, and realize that in reality life never held any meaning for us—except insofar as love, some tiny bit of love, was implicated in some way.

All the rest in that changeover to our recognition of love turns out to be detail. Sometimes painful. Sometimes joyful. At times, it appears even to be a gamble—especially at the beginning. But, we have to take it step-by-step, testing love's new strength, finding its new perspectives. The shape of our life and all in it, we find, changes slowly, imperceptibly. Even the hurt that others may give us we can diminish and eventually overcome. When we can manage to answer hurt in some loving way, we are sharing love even more. We are offering Love Itself, Jesus, to those who hurt us.

"It's your choice." Mary's voice was very soft. "Love won't ever force you. Its hand will never pull back from you. But you must reach out and take it. If you do, all human love will be changed for you forever. No miracles, though. Only that one. The miracle of love. And, in time, it will change your whole world.

"But it's your choice."

Mary rose and reached down. She offered Laura the hand that Love had once taken and made its own forever.

Laura looked upward. Her eyes were shining. She put her hand in Mary's.

❋

"Goodnight ma'am," George opened the door for Mary, and she gave him a smile that warmed his heart.

As she walked away, Mary heard him begin to sing a little ballad to himself. Funny, it just popped into his mind. He hadn't thought of that one in years. Mary could just catch the first words before she was out of earshot.

"You're nobody till somebody loves you . . ."

"Somebody does," Mary said.

The Miraculous Gift

LOVE OF HUSBAND AND WIFE

When Michael and Karen S., the attractive couple in the tenth-floor condominium apartment, let it be known that their marriage was in serious trouble, it came as a shock to many who had known them since their wedding ten years before. Michael and Karen had been envied, in the good sense of the word, by many of their friends. Theirs had seemed an almost perfect partnership from the beginning. But to visit them now, at the low point of their marriage, gave you something of the feeling you have when you visit a ballroom the morning after a celebration. It's filled with vivid reminders of movement and lights and excitement and joy. But they are only reminders.

That's what it had been between Karen and Michael, a partnership full of celebration, an agreement between two people who were already very good friends to tie the knot and make a go of it. They didn't want any other arrangement—no live-in lovers they; no long-standing affair for them; and no so-called open marriage, either before or after they exchanged vows. No. They wanted "a real marriage" with all the promises made and accepted. Why?

Well, the sum of it, they said, was that they were in love and they wanted to have that love all their lives, "Till death do us part."

There were other motives, too. Karen was resolved not to make the errors her mother had made. Her mother's first marriage had been what Karen humorously—well, almost humorously—called a 3-K marriage: kids, kitchen, kirk. When Karen's mother escaped that slavery by divorce, she, and perhaps Karen, too, understood that she had been married to the kind of man who, by that time, finally had been given a name, a public label—chauvinist. But almost at once she entered what Karen and everybody else recognized as an addictive marriage—marriage with a man, that is, who was as addicted to her as some people are to a drug. It appeared almost to be her unplanned revenge for years of unhappiness and forebearance. For, as mad as he was for her, she was unresponsive to him; only, she did enjoy his inherited wealth.

He took her attitude as a sign of strength and independence, and at first it seemed to make up for some weakness in him. But as the marriage progressed, Karen watched her mother become a walking mine of selfish egotism, slowly destroying whatever shred of manhood there was in her second husband. They maintained the facade, however.

Karen, as sensible as she was modern, could see that her mother was doing to her second husband what Karen's father had done. To Karen, one chauvinism did not seem any better than the other.

Michael had no such passionate maelstrom in his background. An only son, he was the product of what he called a celibate marriage. A marriage without any love. His parents, shortly after his birth, found they had absolutely nothing in common with each other. But for family reasons as well as social and religious ones, they decided to stay together as celibates, much as brother and sister. By mutual and discreet consent, they went their separate ways now and again. They, too, maintained the facade, however.

Michael and Karen wanted nothing of the nonsense and make-believe and pretense that, in such different ways, had marked the marriages of their parents.

When they started off their adult lives, each one was what is called a very aware person. They both played the field; they both acquired some experience; and they both knew what they wanted, knew what sort of a person they wanted to spend the rest of their lives with.

Let's start with basics. She preferred rather shorter men, men who were stocky, muscular, a bit hairy, and, of course, not empty-headed. She expected her man to have a profession or a good career. Michael was all of that.

Michael's preferences fell into the same sort of balance sheet, but on the feminine side of the ledger. He preferred blond-haired, long-legged women with regular features, women who weren't spineless "stay-at-homes," women with a certain flair and adventuresomeness—what he called the Yankee type. Karen was all of that for him.

On a more intimate level, they both had the same idea of what a marriage partner should be: Someone who desired to make love with you. No coldness when it was over. No let-down feeling of "so-that's-all-there-is-to-it" boredom. Rather, a feeling of "it's-not-over-with—imagine, this again and again, endlessly!"

Of course, they considered marriage on the broader

social level, too. That was very important if they were going to avoid the mistakes of their elders. Marriage, they knew, was a mode of living that precluded the horrors of being single. Precluded any need to search for a night of excitement that held no other meaning. It precluded that frenetic stalking of enjoyment, that sort of expectant loneliness and frustration the single person must undergo. But, most important, it meant a companion to share the good things of life with.

As to those good things of life, Michael and Karen discussed them all—likes and dislikes in food and friends, and entertainment; the sort of vacations they enjoyed; the money they expected to have at their disposal; their long-range plans for "later on"—that vague time. And, yes, their careers. Michael's position—already a regional manager in an electronics company—assured him of a great future. Karen, with a degree in commercial design, was already on her way in one of the biggest advertising agencies of the country. They found, as the sociologists would say, almost perfect convergence under every heading. Even to their ages: there was just five years' difference, twenty-nine and twenty-four. They both liked that.

So everything was perfect. Karen was everything Michael wanted. And for her, Michael was the man she had always dreamed of marrying. Even the decision to marry was perfect—each of them blurted out a proposal to the other at just the same moment. They laughed happily at that, and they said "yes" and laughed again and hugged. And they knew they were asking each other to merge their already very similar life-styles into one, to have a pairing of likes and wishes and inclinations where the contributions of each harmonized and fused with those of the other. A lovely partnership. A love-full partnership! All in all, life promised so much for them.

They so enjoyed making their plans after that, it was wonderful to see them at it. They would be close friends and partners, sharing all those common interests and likes and goods. They would even have a child, perhaps two— but only after they enjoyed themselves a little more and established themselves financially. So, then, they would be parents! That made them laugh together, too, when they thought about it a little.

And, above all, they would be married—they would achieve that marvelous autonomy, be sufficient unto each other, orbit alone together around the sun of their enjoyment, independent of everyone else, self-sufficient, self-contained, self-satisfying.

They put all of that together into a marriage solemnized one sunny Saturday afternoon in church, blessed by families and friends. A marriage between two mature young adults who came from loveless homes and who were determined there would be love in their marriage. You can't fault anyone for thinking that theirs was a marriage "made in heaven" and certainly as promising as any human undertaking could be.

Successes and joys were theirs, no mistake about it. A year or so after their marriage, they were able to move into a condo apartment. Both were doing well in their careers. They already had a rewarding circle of friends, a way of life and of loving in which each responded perfectly to the other just as they had thought when they had talked for hours and planned it all. Life was good and fun.

When Karen was twenty-seven, they decided to have that child. And it was a girl! Just what both of them wanted! They called her Anne Marie, and her arrival greatly changed their daily existence. That was only to be expected. In fact, they had talked it all out, as they always had done.

At about the same time, Michael's career was opening up on to a wider plane. He became a vice-president and was definitely in line for a place at the long table of the board of directors. After that, who knew how far he might go!

So Karen arranged to work part-time. She made up her mind, with Michael's help, that she should be first and foremost a good mother and then a top-notch illustrator in her field. Still, Michael was able to take Karen with him on *some* of his business trips, when company regulations allowed it or company politics demanded it. In the main, however, he traveled without her.

Both Michael and Karen understood that this was a time for building, for sacrifice, for extra effort while they had that invaluable asset—youth. By middle age, if all went well, they both would have wider and better options. Meanwhile, there was nothing to worry about. Hadn't they talked it all out? Didn't they always?

Perhaps it was true that Michael's world was highly technical, demanding utter concentration on strange formulas and new devices—had even a language all its own. But Karen took all that intelligently and well; she teased her handsome young husband and his colleagues good-naturedly now and again. "When you over-educated Americans get together, you start speaking Eskimo," she would laugh; the terms they used and their snip-snap mode of thinking sounded as strange as that to her.

Laughter or no, now and again Karen had a little secret twinge of fear. In her work, it was the artistic line, the tasteful design, the sensually elegant solution, the catchy slogan matching the design that mattered to her. Michael more often than not seemed to notice only what he called the "slogan-mill" mentality of her world of advertising. He would make funny but biting jokes about the concoction of "selling-lines" and of commercial tags. It wasn't a constant thing. Nothing to worry about. Only— sometimes, just sometimes, Karen felt they might be growing apart. Just a little. Ever so gradually.

For his part, Michael never had that impression. Only —now and again, when he returned home from one of his business trips, he noticed a—what should he call it?—a contrast between the way Karen thought, the way she talked about things, and the way his colleagues thought and spoke. Still, it was nothing to worry about. His deep interest had to be in that world of computer efficiency, after all; their plans, his and Karen's, depended a great deal on his success in that world. They had talked about all that. It was no one's fault if that world attracted a certain type of person, male or female. "Almost a club of their own," Karen thought once or twice. She tried not to think of it very often.

Although at the beginning of their marriage, Karen and Michael would have denied it, their all-important motive for marrying was that each felt satisfied with the other. Each made the other feel good, feel better than they imagined they would be without the other. Of course, neither of them was naive. They both knew that these things change, that their mutual attraction would evolve—they hoped into something just as good or even better. And, anyway, who at the age of twenty or twenty-five, even thirty, can really look beyond thirty-five, or forty? Or who wants to? Is there really anything beyond forty to interest a young person? Especially if you think, as you normally do at that age, that you'll never be old? Karen and Michael knew that things would change. They just didn't suspect that change could mean collapse of their mutual attraction, of their "feeling good about it all," about every bit of the marriage.

It really did seem that there was "nothing to worry about," at least for two or three years after Anne Marie's birth. Only—somewhere along their way together, one day, one night, on this or that occasion, it seemed to one of them, or to both of them—who could be sure by then?—that they faced each other from opposite sides of a narrow crevasse opening between them. Once it was there, it seemed to be widened by almost anything, whether trivial or important. Michael might seem distant in the evening when he could not get his mind off that program he had set up for the new company machine; his partner on that job had made some good contributions. A really intelligent woman, that.

Or perhaps Karen seemed to be getting moody. Michael wondered occasionally if taking care of their two-year-old plus her career was too much for Karen to handle. But Karen didn't complain much and Michael did have his own worries.

And so they walked their increasingly separate ways, barely noticing as the distance increased. Until one day, about ten years into the marriage, the narrow crevasse had become a wide chasm. Suddenly, in fact, it was the Grand Canyon. They tried to talk, even to shout at each other across that unbridgeable gulf. But hearing was difficult, listening next to impossible. Real communication could not reach across so wide a space. And, of course, any whisper of tender love was lost in the deepening shadows that began to fill that canyon between them. All that earlier optimism and joy and satisfaction had, somehow or other, tumbled over the edge of that chasm. They didn't know exactly where. And they couldn't retrace their steps. The partnership was in mortal danger.

When finally they could deny the problem no longer, it was not surprising that they faced it separately. Karen confided first in a woman who had been a girlhood friend of hers; Michael talked with the colleague who was closest to him in the office. It wasn't long, however, before other friends and then still others were aware that there was "some problem between Karen and Michael S."

The threatened shipwreck of this marriage was most poignant and inexplicable for those who had known both of them since before the marriage. "How," they asked each other, "could that marriage, of all marriages, have gone wrong?" Oh, they all knew about all the studies, all the statistics and the theories of sociology and psychology that explain everything nowadays. They all knew the almost fifty-fifty odds between marriages that last and marriages that don't. "But how," they would shake their heads again and repeat sadly, "how could that marriage, of all marriages, have gone wrong?"

"It's something in the air, something in our culture and our age," some would say with a helpless feeling. "Besides," others added, "people are living longer, much longer today. And the choices are greater than ever before. Times are just changing. That's all. It's a pity . . ."

But, for Karen and Michael, talk about culture and the

age we live in was just too cold. Changing times were not a surprise, but neither were they an explanation, and certainly no help. They had planned to keep changing, together, with the times. They knew what sort of marriage they had intended from the beginning. Fifty-fifty, indeed! They had a better chance of success than that.

.Well, hadn't they always—at least at the start—talked everything out between them? Why not get someone to help them do that again? A professional. A marriage counselor. The best. One of the real experts who study these things for a living.

The man they finally chose explained it to them. There is, he said, a funny thing about the heart, the emotions. Despite your best intentions, there are certain needs of the heart that cannot be pushed aside or swept under the rug, he said. When the heart goes cold over one person, he said; or when sexual attraction really flags and gets boring or does not really provide a "high," he said; or when someone other than your partner really comes to mean something special and the old marriage is just tooling along with all the usual ups and downs, he said; when any one or all of these conditions apply, he said, then the heart is sending out a vital signal.

What it all came down to was very practical. If that magnificent feeling of wanting to be one with your partner faded or stopped altogether, well, what could a person do? You are, after all, your compulsions. A bundle of them. Oh, call it your heart, if you prefer. But that's only the poetic word for a very unpoetic, hard-nosed, measurable need in each one of us: To be ourselves.

"And," the expert said, "ultimately, a person has no

real control over that bundle of compulsions that make up the most intimate self each one of us is. In fact, it can be very dangerous if we deny those compulsions for too long." He told Karen and Michael of some very sad cases—depression, violence, worse. It was often dangerous not "to satisfy the heart, if you want to speak romantically," he said.

Michael and Karen paid the expert his fee, and he wished them good luck. They thanked him. He had been generous with his time, after all; and if all his studies and all his wisdom made it seem that even fifty-fifty odds of success in marriage today are too optimistic by far, well, at least they had tried.

And whose fault was it if, when they left that office after their last consultation, they walked sadly back to their car, still on opposite sides of their personal Grand Canyon? What expert could possibly have so good a map as to find for them some tiny path that they could not find alone, some little opening, that would lead them back together again?

The most curious thing, it seems to me, and by far the saddest, is that no one Karen and Michael went to for help, no friend and no expert, spoke about or even recalled what Jesus, who is Love itself, taught us about love and about marriage. It seemed that neither they nor anyone they knew had ever dreamed, or acknowledged the tiniest memory, that the very meaning of married love is a union far grander than any mere partnership; or that it reaches far beyond the enjoyment and independence and satisfaction and autonomy that Michael and Karen had imagined would be the deepest rewards of their life together; or that it is perhaps the closest mirror of the Love in which all love has not only its meaning, but its very existence.

Instead, what they had been told was that "until death do us part" did not mean until their own deaths, but until the death of their attraction to one another. If you looked at it that way, the way the experts did, "until death do us part" was not a vow, but an escape hatch, a promise meant to last until attraction eddied away. Or until something more attractive might weave a newer spell, suggest a different promise, supplant the outworn vow. They had been told that they should regard love as an absolute right, not as a gift, and certainly not as the mirror of the divine in human existence. No. Love's meaning, as they could read in any of a dozen current books, is that "bundle of needs and compulsions that we are only beginning to understand."

It all came down to a sad truth, but truth it seemed to be. Michael and Karen only had to look around them. In magazines, in those books, on television, in films—everywhere—love is presented as an absolute right. It is something you create with another person. If that person fails you, then there is, in this enlightened time, a right to change. You owe it to yourself.

Just suppose, I wondered to myself, that Michael and Karen S. could find another kind of friend, a couple whose miraculous wedding gift was another vision. Just suppose that Michael and Karen could walk into the lives of another pair, in another time, the way they walk into a movie and are willingly, for that while, drawn into someone else's world.

It's not hard to imagine. You may remember, as I do,

that film, *Rebecca*, made from the novel by Daphne du Maurier. The film began with a view of a burned-out, abandoned skeleton of a once fine mansion, overgrown now with weeds and ivy. A woman's voice began the story. Manderly, that mansion was called, she told us. Once it stood proud and beautiful on the Cornish coast. And, as she spoke, the film took us back, as if by magic, to an earlier time. The ruins on the screen began to change, became again a glistening place set, on a bright spring morning, in its own woods and well-kept gardens.

In just such a way I would, if I could, draw Karen and Michael into another time, into a different story where the answer they want and need so much to find, lies waiting for them. It's not hard to imagine . . .

❅

"Cana lies in ruins now, as you can see. You can still tell where the main square was, and there are traces still of the paving stones that lined Cana's streets and squares. But once upon a time this was not a pile of ruins."

Michael and Karen had gotten in just in time. Parking the car and then waiting in that line for popcorn had delayed them a little. The theater was already dim, but it appeared to be small.

As they settled into their seats, there was something just a little odd. Maybe it was something about that voice-over, or the camera technique. It almost seemed as if there were no separation between themselves and the images they watched. Maybe it was just that they had come in to the cinema in just the right mood.

Unlike my example of *Rebecca*, this story they were watching was real. A documentary. Or, more exactly, a recreation. The voice-over was already moving on and quickly captured their full attention. They forgot about that oddness.

"There was a time—our time, Aquila's and mine—" (the voice was a woman's) "—when Cana was a magnificent town, the envy of most other towns in Galilee, except perhaps for Magdala."

Karen and Michael watched as the images of gray ruins were transformed perfectly in time with the voice-over. "Turn left here with me," the voice told them. "Look! There! That row of masonry was once the magnificent outer wall of the house where I was married. And those columns—there were fifteen of them then—supported the great walls of the family residence. And just there, at the center of the cobblestone courtyard, was a fountain of the clearest water. It was perfect for celebration, for dancing. And that spring morning of the day of our wedding, guests were everywhere, laughing and sharing the joy.

"And more guests arrived every moment, it seemed. As each new one arrived, the stewards gave them the traditional welcome, dipping a shallow cup into one of the six huge jars of fresh water and pouring the water over the fingers of each guest. Finally, almost everyone we knew and some we didn't were there, the water jars were quite empty, and the stewards hurried about other tasks."

The images changed with every word. Each phrase was like a wand restoring before the eyes of Michael and Karen the very scene of that marriage feast at Cana. The walls were whole again. Water splashed and played in the courtyard fountain, catching sunlight in its drops. People appeared everywhere, walking and sitting and chatting, gossiping and laughing. There was music. Waiters and stewards bustled about the place. It was almost too real. Michael and Karen felt they could reach out and take a cup of wine, move among the guests, trace a hand in the cool fountain. They were like privileged but unseen guests mingling with the others there.

"A toast! A toast!" All heads turned, Michael's and Karen's too, as the bride and groom came into the sunlight. "To Aquila and Priscilla! Long, long life!" Every voice took up the traditional toast. Every hand raised a glass of wine. "To Aquila! To Priscilla! Long, long life!"

They were a fine-looking bride and bridegroom. Young. Both of them beautiful. Happiness heightened the radiance of Priscilla's cheeks as she spoke with this guest and that, thanking one for a gift, laughing with another, just as Karen had done 2,000 years later at her own marriage. Michael and Karen recognized Priscilla's as the voiceover that had transformed the sad deserted ruins of Cana into this living, moving place on such a happy occasion.

Aquila, too, made the rounds among the guests, joked with old friends. Hadn't they had times together! All kinds of carousing and parties—not all as correct and blessed as this one, either! A man in his twenties was expected to taste life before he settled down, after all. Later he would have to be more discreet—or so the jokes went there in the happy sunshine. Michael laughed with the rest. These friends of Aquila were so like those old buddies he had joked with at his and Karen's wedding.

Aquila and Priscilla wove in and out among the guests, and then came together in the courtyard or under a portico and stayed together a little before going back to their social duties, accepting more toasts, welcoming latecomers to the celebration. After quite a while, though,

Aquila began to look toward the door leading to the inner courtyard. The sun was already high. Surely it was past time for the head caterer to remove the veal and lamb from the huge roasting spits in the kitchen, and to call the family and close friends to be served, while the many other guests ate their fill from the endless platters that would be provided for them.

Just as he called a steward over, ready to send him to find the caterer—to sober him up probably, Aquila thought—so that the feast could begin, he noticed a little scene between a woman friend of his mother's and a younger man Aquila knew was her son. It was strange that it should have caught his eye like that, because there was nothing hurried or strange in what they were doing. Maybe that was it: The contrast they provided to all the noise and movement.

Michael and Karen knew the pair. As if they had seen that mother and that son every day of their lives. Mary— who looked as Michael and Karen had always known she would, although neither had ever really thought about it— leaned to where her son, Jesus, was sitting—and he looked just as Karen and Michael had always known he would. . . .

Mary said something to Jesus, and she gestured toward a wine jar.

"There is no more wine left." Karen and Michael whispered to each other the words they remembered from John's account of this day in his Gospel.

Aquila followed Mary's gesture. He saw the wine jar. And—at last!—the head caterer standing beside it with a very worried look on his face. A few more quiet words passed between Mary and her son, as Aquila made his way to where the caterer stood. Then Mary gestured to a steward who approached her; he listened, and looked puzzled when she pointed to six empty earthenware jars that stood to one side. But he did what he was told. Shrugging his shoulders as if to ask "What next?" he called for some waiters to fill the six jars with water.

Shortly, all was as Mary knew it should be. And everyone, Aquila among them now, waited. It was indeed strange. It seemed to make no sense to scurry about filling jars with water. Yet, not only was it done, now there was a little group of people gathered about, watching as if they too were asking, "What next?"

"Draw a cupful from one jar," Jesus said to the waiter, "and carry it to the caterer there."

It wasn't a moment before that astonished man, all worry banished, all smiles instead, rushed up to Aquila, admiration and compliments on this finest of wines pouring from his lips. "Why, any host but Aquila would never dream of serving such wine to guests who—no offense, you understand—have had enough good wine to be content now with a worse brand. But you have kept the finest wine until now!"

A puzzled Aquila took the cup of wine the head caterer held out to him, tasted its extraordinary rich, smooth flavor. He was so astonished that he was dumbstruck. He could say nothing. The half-full wine glass still near his lips, Aquila raised his eyes to look at Jesus. And he found Jesus looking back at him, a lovely smile, or a golden light that seemed a smile, in his eyes.

"It was strange." A voice-over again, clearly Aquila's this time. "It was strange, but what drew me at that precise second was not the miracle that Jesus had done for us. That got my attention, yes. But what drew me was that smile, that light—how can I say it?—something that reached out like Love itself and drew me toward—well, I couldn't have told you toward what! Not then, anyway. But whatever it was, I wanted it. Not greedily, as you want gold. And not just for myself. But for the new self Priscilla and I would become.

"And that was strange too. I had never in my life had a thought like that. But there it was, complete and new and shining in my mind, and I went to find my bride and bring her to answer the smile of Jesus with me."

Michael and Karen watched as the images changed before them again, fitting themselves to the words Aquila spoke. Aquila quickly found Priscilla in the crowd, whispered to her, and took her by the hand.

Jesus had sat down again by the time Aquila was back with Priscilla. There was a small group of men around Jesus—obviously his companions.

"One of them, Nathaniel," Aquila's voice-over continued, "was from Cana, and I knew him. The others I would come to know in time."

"We both would." That was Priscilla's voice again. "But that first time, we did little more than listen. I don't know for how long. It seemed a moment. But when that moment was over, everything was changed. The way we saw each other. The way we saw marriage. The way we saw love. But really, I guess it was the other way around. First, the way we saw love—*that* changed. Everything else follows from love."

"The first words Jesus actually spoke to us," Aquila's voice returned, "were going to be a toast—or so I thought. Because he raised his cup, filled with that incomparable wine. And that voice, when I heard it, was like a mirror that reflected all the meaning that life requires. And yet, it was not a strange voice at all. It's very hard to put it into words. But I think somehow you needn't have been there to understand. Isn't that odd?"

Michael and Karen did not think it was odd. They understood. At this moment, they seemed to understand. They watched, with no distance at all, it seemed, between them and Aquila and Priscilla and Jesus.

Cup held out to them at first, Jesus spoke quietly to the young couple. "This," he said, "if you choose, will be the story of your love for one another." He drank some wine, and put the glass down. "You may think you know what love is." Jesus looked at Aquila first. "And you," he turned to Priscilla, "may have waited for the day when you would learn love in your husband's arms. But I tell you that love is something you will learn together. And, if you choose, and if you are true to the choice, you will drink the sweetest wine of love at the very moment when you think there is no wine left."

So spellbound were those about Jesus that their silence became like a little eddy flowing outward, a quiet signal silencing the talk and the clatter all over the courtyard, and seeming to gather all the guests, Karen and Michael among them, closer about.

"The wine your waiters pour now is a sign of my Father's pleasure. Of my Father's blessing." Jesus did not seem to raise his voice; but everyone could hear him. "But it is more. It is a sign for you of where love comes from. For love has a source, unchanging and forever. And it is not in your bodies. Love is of my Father. As this wine is of my Father."

Jesus spoke of so many things in the happy tranquillity

of that place. His words seemed to freshen the heart, to open the mind to a new dimension that was not cluttered with puzzles, yet discovered meaning with ease. Michael and Karen lost all track of time. As Priscilla had said, it seemed but a moment.

"Love, all love," Jesus told them, "belongs to my Father. It begins with him, and it has all its meaning and its fulfillment in him." A strange thought, at first, for most of the people there. Mary, his mother, understood, and maybe some of those men who had come with Jesus understood. Maybe. But for the rest of his listeners, Jesus was very patient.

They all knew, Jesus reminded them, of God's law given through Moses: A man shall leave his father and his mother, and be with his wife, and they shall be as one. Yes, they all remembered that. Michael even thought he remembered those very words in their own wedding ceremony, his and Karen's. But in the next moment, Jesus showed how that law had been twisted and the meaning wrung out of it, so that more and more people became more and more certain that husband and wife are one, one body, that is to say, when they lie together. And somehow, with that ease and freshness of understanding, he led them to see that such an idea is a bodily idea only; that if you believe such a thing, you are bound to live for the flesh only, for your compulsions only. . . .

"And then," Jesus asked, "what of my Father? Will you turn away from him? Or will you hear what Moses heard? Will you hear not only Moses' words, but Moses' meaning? God's meaning? For," Jesus said, "Moses saw and described spirit, not flesh."

How can flesh be that which unites wife and husband?

Jesus mocked the very idea. Is their flesh not separate? Are their bodies not two bodies? Moses was not a fanciful man. He did not speak in symbols. If he had meant one in flesh, if he had understood that from the Father, then that is how it would be. But everyone can see around them men and women who have been husbands and wives for many years. They go their separate ways each morning. One may be absent for days. For weeks. They are very separate in that way. And, if their only union is in the flesh, it is no union at all, but only a plague of yearning and loneliness among men and women.

Nothing, Jesus assured them, has been made except by the Father. The man or woman who does not see that, or who decides to turn away from that most basic of all facts, will turn away from all meaning, and in solitude will face the fears and great pain that will start again with every dawning day.

So then, how *can* a woman and a man be as one? Only by union with spirit. Not only in spirit, but with the Spirit sent by the Father, and announced that day and on other days in many ways by his Son. The Father created humankind in his own image, and he created male and female. Neither apart from the other is complete; together they are complete only if they are united as well with the Spirit that is not some airy buzz-word, but is God himself. That is the gift that brings ordinary men and women the closest they may ever come on Earth to the object of all their living desire—Love.

Still, this union is not a magic thing. It does not happen because a man and woman stand together before an altar. It happens because they ask for it to happen; because they intend for it to happen in their lives and between themselves; and because their love, created in spirit, will be nurtured and celebrated in that same Spirit's domain. Physical love is but one celebration of love. If it becomes the only act of love, however, it ceases to be love at all. It becomes mere desire. It is called lust. And that is why, Jesus said, a man can look at his own wife with lust. And that is not love. "Husbands. Love your wives," Paul would echo this truth on another day, "as Christ loved his Church. It is a great mystery . . ."

Love, then, is a gift. It is from God. It is not merited. It is expected, because we come to expect everything God has given, and because his gifts form the very conditions in which life is at all possible. The great mistake is made when men and women turn all that upside down, when they insist that the means God has given them to share in his very life are taken for the final goal.

"That," Jesus told them, picking up his wine glass again, "is like emptying the wine from this glass." And he poured out the rich, red liquid, his miraculous wedding gift to Aquila and Priscilla, and let it run onto the stones at his feet to dry quickly in the sun, until no trace of it was left. "If you do that—and you can choose to, no one will stop you—the only treasure you then possess is the vessel from which the wine was to be drunk."

That, Jesus said to them all, was why he had told Aquila he had not yet learned about love, even as Priscilla had not. Even as many who had been married long since, still had not. They should not waste the wine of love given them as a gift by God. They should not treasure only the vessel of the flesh in which it was given to them to love. If they accepted his words on this, Jesus promised them, then the sweetest wine, still beyond their imagining, was yet to be drunk by them. And even those vessels that seem to be empty, as those earthen jars had been empty before his miracle, even those could be filled again by the miracle of transforming love. On one simple condition; they must have the will, the real and honest will, to do so. For, then, they would see beyond the physical contours of love and recognize the image they are privileged to create by their married love.

In the brief years that followed the marriage feast of Cana, Jesus taught many things about love; in that little theater of their yearning for what they had dreamed their own marriage would be, Karen and Michael saw many of them in the company of that couple of Jesus' time.

"We followed him after that," Aquila's voice told them. "We were his disciples from that day onward. We could not be with him every moment, though we would have liked that. He had given us a different vocation. But we were among the many who would find him wherever he was. Whenever we could, we would spend days or weeks in his company. In Capernaum. In Bethany. In Jerusalem . . ."

Each place Aquila named appeared before Karen and Michael as it was in that ancient time. In each place they were with Jesus, with Priscilla and Aquila, as they had been at the wedding feast, seeing what they saw, hearing what they heard. Scenes of towns and cities, of crowds, of vicious enemies, of lonely vigils. Jesus preaching of love and its demands and its rewards, feeding five thousand people by multiplying five loaves and a few fishes into a bounteous meal. A blind man who suddenly could see. A leper whose skin became fresh as a child's again. A man crippled since birth who leaped about with joy. Martha grieving for her dead brother, Lazarus. Lazarus, beloved friend of Jesus, raised from the grave and appearing at the mouth of the tomb still wrapped in his shroud.

Each miracle said to Karen and Michael that love is greater than anything we can imagine. Water into wine? No one could possibly do that? Love *did* that. And love *does* that. All the time. Water into wine. Grief into joy. Death into life.

"It appeared to us at first," Priscilla spoke again, "that Jesus simply happened to be in this or that place at a particular moment. That a blind man or a leper or a cripple just happened across his path, and that he felt pity. But we lived longer on Earth than Jesus did, and in time we pieced it all together with the bright knowledge of faith and truth we had learned from him. We came to know it was not chance. Nothing just happens.

"That was a huge realization for us. You see, it meant that in all the miracles Jesus performed, he deliberately revealed his Father's will and his union with his Father. More than once we heard him say: 'I and the Father are one. I do this so that you may believe, and be one with me and with the Father.'

"And of all the miracles he performed, the miracle at Cana was his first. We should really speak of his miracles at Cana. For there was more than one. Not merely water into wine. But the union of man and woman into a sacrament. The truth he revealed by that miracle was the greatest miracle of all. The truth he unveiled was the wine offered at *each* marriage.

"And that truth is this: Jesus' choice to be present at Cana before he did all the other things meant that he placed marriage before all other human endeavors—with the sole exception of the work he called his Apostles to do. He revealed marriage to be a holy thing. A sacrament, it has always been called by the Church since then. And so it is.

"And, furthermore, the truth is this: that the vows between a man and a woman when they celebrate that sacrament, are vows shared with God. They are vows that say, 'Yes Lord, we know love is your gift. And we take it from your hands to share with one another. We know by your gift that we are not like animals who come together with no knowledge of your purpose, no gift of your Spirit, no agreement before you, God, to love with your Love.'

"And the truth is this: Only in the sacred union of marriage do men and women mirror the completeness of God. For that union, that sacrament, is a mirror of his love joined with his will, each possessed completely by the other. That union is the bedrock of all else we do. Our motives, our drives, our labor, our children, our nations, our world, all derive their continuing strength, and their strength to continue, from that union—if we are as true to the promise we make to each other and to God, as God has given us reason to be.

"Yet, make no mistake. The truth is also this: It is not always easy to be true. We, Aquila and Priscilla, learned that. But we also learned that love and its purposes are not weakling things. Jesus, who is God, and who came to Cana and showed in the bright morning sun of this world the importance of love in the very life and mind of God, that same Jesus showed us, too, how love was willing to suffer. He showed us how much pain love can endure. He showed us how nothing, not persecution, not living hate, not death itself, is stronger than love. No scourging, no punishment,

however undeserved, no cross, is enough to force love and
its purpose aside—if that love is always offered to God with
the prayer that it be strengthened with his very love, and
used for his very purpose, in his very will.

"And the truth is finally this: As with every offer of
love made to us by God, we can refuse it; or we can play
with it for a while, and then turn to other things. But if we
do, then let us never say love has abandoned us, that there
is no more love in our world. We need never ask: Is there
still love? For love there always is. Love's offer is the only
offer that is eternal, that never dies, that never fails, is
never withdrawn, that is stronger than death itself. If followed, love unites us finally with God."

Priscilla's voice fell silent. There were only images before Karen and Michael, making it appear that they were
drawing back to a point from which they could take in a
great panorama, see everything in perspective. They saw
Cana again, lying on the shores of Galilee. And they saw
that lake as a landmark in that whole privileged land; and
that whole land as the one place on Earth where Love
Itself was born as a human baby, was cared for by the most
perfect husband and wife who ever lived, and finally tri-
umphed over death. Very near the center of that panorama, in which "the eyes of the heart are enlightened to
see how great is the hope to which we are called in Christ
Jesus," they saw the cup offered by the hand of God. And
the sweet wine that filled that cup was the love of God
Himself.

❈

Whose fault was it if, when Michael and Karen left the
marriage expert's office and walked disconsolately back to

their car, they still were on opposite sides of their personal Grand Canyon? What expert could, by then, find for them some tiny path that would lead them back together?

As they drove toward home, disappointed, perhaps the only hopeful sign was that each of them still yearned for the special closeness they had once thought their marriage would bring them. Heaven knows, Michael thought to himself, they had tried. Maybe that was part of it. Maybe they had been trying too hard lately, talking to too many friends and too many experts.

He glanced at Karen sitting beside him, lost in her own thoughts. She looked as weary as he felt.

He looked back at the road again. Up ahead, just a block away, he noticed a movie marquee. Why not? Maybe a little relaxation, an evening together, just the two of them, the way they used to spend evenings together— dinner, a movie, a stroll. Maybe that would ease things a little. A first step, anyway.

He looked more closely at the movie marquee as they drove by in the slow traffic. "LAURENCE OLIVIER FESTIVAL," it said. "TONIGHT: REBECCA."

That was an old favorite of theirs. Above the marquee was one of those banners they use for special announcements. Michael craned his neck to read it. "SNEAK PREVIEW: SMASH NEW DOCUMENTARY-SAGA. TONIGHT ONLY."

Well, a bit of the old and a bit of the new! Why not? he thought again. He glanced at Karen, just as she had caught sight of the name *Rebecca*. The hint of a smile he used to see all the time began to play around her mouth.

"Why not?" she said his own thought to him.

Chaplain and
the Battle of "Why Not?"

PERSONAL LOVE AND FRIENDSHIP

WITH JESUS

FOR as long as anyone could remember, everyone had always just called him Chaplain. Not the way you would call a stranger in uniform "Lieutenant," of course. Nothing of that sort. No. He didn't merely fill a post. It was more that Chaplain *was* what he did.

He was different in other ways, as well. For one thing he never seemed to be a stranger. From the first moment of your first meeting with him, when he turned that craggy face your way, those eyes that were both kind and piercing pulled aside all curtains of unknowing and of pretense. Yet he was never intrusive or prying.

Another thing about Chaplain was that, churchman or no, he was a realist. He had seen just about everything, good, and bad, and no one ever accused him of having his head in the clouds. In fact, after some forty years as university chaplain on the same campus, it seemed as though the greater part of several generations had come to him with very real, very tough problems. Everyone knew that you could "talk anything over with Chaplain."

"Chaplain!" a student would catch up with him as he walked across campus, "I really need some help." "Orrite," Chaplain would answer—it was a funny little mannerism of speech he had—"orrite, come by today if you can. We'll talk."

Or it might be a professor or a dean stopping by to see him. Or a worried mother and father, former students themselves, perhaps, calling about their own children who were students now. Or it might be the campus gardener or a janitor who needed some help, some word of guidance. There were thousands who had gone to Chaplain over those years, to talk and cry and laugh and find a special sort of aid. In their poverty and their ambitions, in their doubts and their mistakes. Brilliance and stupidity, laziness and crime and cheating and jealousy and cruelty all marched across campus—as they do across life—and right into Chaplain's little office. He saw drug problems and alcohol problems and poverty problems and too-much-money problems and sex problems. He had even seen murder. There was no one who could not go to Chaplain, and very few who didn't.

Now, with all of that, you would expect any man, even a saint, to become hardened and harried and glum, maybe display a tinge of the cynical and bitter. But Chaplain was different in that respect, too. And that was probably the biggest difference between him and others.

"One of the facts that most baffles non-Christians," Chaplain often mused with an old friend from time to time, "is the Christian belief that each one of us is called to lead a personal life united with Jesus. Anyone who thinks that Christianity is just supposed to be a set of rules for ethical conduct, or a set of abstract beliefs to be accepted by the mind like a geographer's map or a chemist's table of the elements or a new 'language' to make a computer work —well," and Chaplain would shake his head sadly as though remembering one case or another, "well, anyone who thinks that has missed the one key element that makes it all work: Personal love of Jesus, and personal friendship with him."

Those weren't just words for Chaplain. He really did cultivate Jesus as one person cultivates another. He talked with Jesus in prayer, worshiped him in church, shared his work and his thoughts and just about everybody's problems with Jesus. He bore the pains and failures of life as a small participation in the sufferings of Jesus, and he enjoyed the good things of life as blessings Jesus sends those he loves. When Chaplain encouraged those who came to him "to get to know Jesus, his likes and dislikes," and to "act in everyday matters out of love for Jesus," he was only giving the advice he had followed for all the years he could remember.

There was a lot of muscle, in addition to personal faith and habit and preference, in that kind of advice from Chaplain. He had earned his own university degrees in Bible and Middle Eastern studies. He read the Bible in the original languages. He had long ago traveled and studied in the lands where Jesus and his Apostles had walked and taught. All that preparation gave Chaplain a particular quality that you came to value highly. He could chat about the Apostles and about Jesus and his contemporaries in such a way that you almost had the impression he had spent time with them. He could bring to life the small but significant facts—how they dressed, ate, talked; what their particular ways of expressing themselves were; the meaningful gestures they surely used to convey what they felt. Not like some scholar dripping with information about bygone days and long dead people. In some curious but quite natural way, he seemed to be speaking directly in the presence of Jesus, whom he saw with a special vision—a familiarity, some said—all his own.

So, when Chaplain talked about friendship with Jesus, it wasn't a platitude or a figure of speech. Not by a long shot. And he left no doubt that he meant the real thing: Real, living friendship. And he was tough about it.

"If you want to find out the essentials of loving anyone," he would say, "even yourself, then you have to learn what it is in you that makes possible or impossible the love of Jesus." Then he'd turn those sharp eyes filled with a gentle warning: "The temptation is always to get that backwards. To see Jesus' love as a mirror of your own. That will get you into trouble, nine times out of ten."

And nine times out of ten, that mistake was what brought people to Chaplain. Oh, the details changed from person to person, from year to year, from decade to decade. But most often love and friendship with Jesus was the nub of the matter, and most often, the demand was something like, "my will be done," and "if Jesus forbids me my love, forbids me to love in my way, then Jesus doesn't love me."

Back in the forties, Chaplain could recall, when he was still fairly new at the university himself, there was that huge influx of World War II veterans. They were practical-minded men, older than the students who came before and after them. Most had brushed very close to death and

suffering and fear of an extreme kind. Many had come
through with a toughened faith in Jesus, a gratitude for
having survived, and with some practical demands they
made upon Jesus, and often shared with Chaplain, too.
They had lost time to make up, they told him, dreams they
had fought for and had come home to claim. Quite a few
married while they were still in school—a revolutionary
change in its time—and many came to him for help in the
problems and strains that more typically came after gradu-
ation. Still, while they had many "my-will-be-done" demands they felt Jesus must sanction, must justify, Chaplain
saw quickly that many of them felt a special affinity for
him and for his advice because they, too, each in his own
way, had come to know quite well what it was to have
Jesus as their friend and the sole guarantor of life.

The children of those war veterans, however, were a
different breed, and a change seemed to come with them to
the campus like a sudden wind, a harbinger of storms.
They seemed to know nothing of what their fathers and
mothers had suffered and borne. Out of love, their parents
had handed what they themselves had demanded, as a gift
to their children. The generation of the late fifties, Chaplain thought, was the first in countless centuries to be
given everything. They had been reared to think that to be
American was to have the good life. When they said, in
their turn, "My will be done," they meant cars and houses
and vacations and retirement. And over it all, there was a
certain smugness, a certain arrogance. How many times
had Chaplain said to students in those years, "The good
life is not an aim in itself. If that is your demand, your
whole reason for study and work, then you will find you
are an empty shell by the time you're forty. Buckets of

money do not bring the good life—not the really good life. That comes as a consequence of love. And that comes as a consequence of Jesus' love in your life." As always, some heard what Chaplain was telling them; but some didn't. And Chaplain's warnings were fulfilled, much to his sadness, to such a degree that the label of "quiet desperation" was attached to that generation as it moved in its later years through the unfolding of the empty "good life."

The sixties brought not just more winds, but the storm itself, an explosion of changes, of new demands, of revolt against what many saw as the sterility of the fifties. The good life was not enough. "My will be done" took more strident forms. There were loyalty rallies and crusade rallies. Then rallies against loyalty rallies, and rallies to defend one loyalty against another. There were peace rallies and war rallies. Every sort of slogan began to turn up on banners and signs. And finally "Jesus" rallies began to spring up. Signs bobbed across campuses declaring "Jesus saves!" and "I'm for Jesus." There were even bumper stickers urging you to "Honk for Jesus!" A lot of people began talking about a "new era of liberation" that was dawning with them. Many seemed to understand liberation to mean "anything goes, as long as you really want it, really feel it."

Chaplain worried about that upheaval. It wasn't that some comfortable order of things was changing; change as such did not frighten him. He did not feel cheated or threatened or indignant or insulted, as others did. No, as with most things about Chaplain, his reasons for worry were different.

His first reason was that liberation, the kind that Jesus promised, doesn't work that way. Chaplain's life of inner devotion to Jesus, and all of his reading and experience and knowledge of faith, told him that those who experience Jesus really, those who start to live a life of love for Jesus and of friendship with him, are always marked by certain changes. They become gentler, not more strident—but this does not mean they become weak. Their language searches for ways to convey spirit and its meaning, and so it doesn't become coarser or harder to understand or more vulgar. Rather, they seem to say with David: "Let your faithful ones bless you, Lord. Let them discourse of the glory of your kingdom." They display a greater respect for other people, and dislike offending, even in small things such as dress and ordinary manners—as though, with Paul, they live their lives "worthy of their calling, with respect, humility, meekness and patience, bearing with one another lovingly."

They quickly shed a certain darkness of mind, as though they have been put in touch with all the saints and holy ones who have been known for their devotion to Jesus, and who have always said to Jesus what Jesus said to his Father: "Thy will, not mine, be done."

Chaplain didn't see much sublimity in the new language of the zealous youngsters, nor much reverence in their tones. Not much respect or humility, either. And as for patience, they seemed to want to discard it along with all the other "dumb rules and regulations."

The second reason the frenzies of the sixties worried Chaplain was that more people than ever seemed to be coming to him in impatient confusion and disappointment that they would not admit to anyone else. Some were even in deep depression and despair, wanting to chuck everything, to "drop out." They wept that Jesus wasn't keeping his end of the bargain. The circumstances were vastly different from those of the forties, and even the fifties. But the demand was the same. "My will be done," they each seemed to say in one way or another. "Otherwise, Jesus doesn't love me."

By the seventies, the storm of demands on Jesus had begun to change again. If Jesus loved you, campus zealots declared, he would further your political cause. He would stop the war in Vietnam or free the Third World from capitalistic domination, or stop inflation, or lower taxes, or end the draft, or legalize marijuana, or allow polygamy. He would sweep away authority—civil, religious, whatever kind there was—and free each individual to follow his own lights, his own inner voices, his own "conscience"—though that word had no meaning any longer that Chaplain could recognize.

Chaplain was asked often, over those turbulent years, to attend rally after rally. He would always decline with thanks and a smile. He had found Jesus long before most of these people had been born, had been friends with him all his life, and tested everything he did and saw in the light of that friendship. He knew: You don't look for Jesus at a political rally. You look for him in prayerful solitude, in the church, in the Bible, in your own heart, with a friend, and with solid guidance. But not in frenzies that have something other than Jesus at their center.

It saddened Chaplain, but, again, did not seem to surprise him, that as the fervors changed and increased over the years, more and more people seemed to become as disappointed and confused as the multitudes that tried to make Jesus a king, a political hero, a new David, but found instead that Jesus departed from them in that instant. Just so, these young men and women of the seventies found themselves further and further from the peace and happiness that was their goal.

"It's not that the goal isn't there for you," Chaplain used to say often, though in different ways to different people. "It's just that someone gave you the wrong end of the telescope, and you took it, and your view is totally distorted." It was another way of saying that if you get love's message backwards, it will get you into trouble every time.

Then, as suddenly as the storms of the sixties and seventies had exploded—whop!—they were gone. The eighties dawned in an eerie calm. Some said the turbulence had died, spent itself. But Chaplain knew better. It was like walking through rubble after a tornado. Everyone seemed stunned. All the structures were down and no one seemed to agree on how, or even what, to rebuild. There seemed no blueprints to guide them, the new generation of youngsters said, when they came to see Chaplain now; there was no plan to follow. All they could see from horizon to horizon was a stumbling about in confusion and contradiction. The fitness craze and the drug plague ran side by side. Students jogged in the parks and raised marijuana on their window sills. They talked about love but stalked sex. There arose a clash and a jumble of opposites that was deafening.

A lesser friend of Jesus than Chaplain might have been weary after all he had seen come and go, or at least have been ready for an easier life. He had had, after all, plenty of offers for more honored and certainly less demanding assignments. But he always refused those offers, quoting a phrase the Israelites used when their enemies tried to distract them from building the walls of the Temple. "We are engaged in a great work," he would say, eyes twinkling, "and we cannot come down." How could he walk away from people who needed him, who were accustomed to having him near, and particularly now, when so many looked to him for help in making their way through an uncharted minefield of choices and possibilities?

So, by the time the eighties were underway, Chaplain was practically a one-man institution. In fact, the only thing that never seemed to change on Chaplain's campus was that young people always loved to gather around him. Even when they had no specific problems, they would often come by for a quick hello or a bit of reassurance—just to share in the special light that Chaplain seemed to have and to be able to give away to others, without losing it himself. Though they would not have put it in so many words, the fact was that to be with Chaplain was to feel through him a calm ocean of hope that could have no source in this world merely, and to share in a peace and a courage, a large-mindedness and a tough-mindedness that all seemed to be a promise, a little echo, of what Jesus offers. For, to be with Chaplain was to share in the special ability he had to commune openly with Jesus as a living, listening, helping Lord and friend.

On any early evening in Chaplain's small quarters, there might be six or seven students gathered, talking about anything and everything, holding it all up to that light by which Chaplain tested everything he saw and did. Nothing was off limits in those discussions. The young people who came to see him now regarded all the explosions of the sixties and seventies with some curiosity, but no empathy. Their concerns were not for tearing apart the old. In fact, it seemed to many of them, so much had been torn apart in twenty years, they saw their own problem as trying to find their way on a relatively blank map. When "anything goes" is the only rule, a lot of people get lost.

Pre-law students began to talk with deep feeling about the moral and religious underpinnings of law and what would happen if none were acknowledged. Pre-med students were genuinely concerned over dozens of new issues and decisions they knew they would have to face without much help one of these days as doctors. Business-administration majors raised a host of issues about what they called "bottom-line ethics." Anthropology majors were often troubled by the way their textbooks used religion as just another artifact, "like a thighbone or a clay pot," as one of them said, "to help you figure out migration patterns or some such problem."

Everyone chimed in about all of it. But mostly they were eager to hear Chaplain hold their problems and questions up to the measure Jesus had drawn up for them, to compare their own ideas with what Jesus said or did, what he showed to this Apostle, through that disciple, to a believer or to a non-believer; and what Christians had always held and understood through the centuries.

It was at one of those evening sessions that Chaplain first met Joan C.

It would have been hard not to notice Joan, even in a larger group. She made it clear that she had originally agreed to come along with a friend out of curiosity, to see for herself whether this famous Chaplain she had heard so

much about lived up to his reputation. Chaplain didn't
know if he had passed muster, but he knew Joan must
have found some agreeable spark because she took to showing up quite often.

Chaplain cared about and remembered almost everybody who ever came to him. But there was something special for him about this young woman. Or, perhaps not just
something, but an amalgam of things. It almost seemed to
him that she was the living example of "getting it all
backwards," and of the clashes and confusions of her time.
Instead of having one or two or five goals or desires, or
wishes, Joan had none, because she had them all. In her
own words, she "was not ready to decide." She "had a
healthy curiosity."

"Life is an open field, after all," she challenged Chaplain, "and I don't see anything wrong with roaming over as
much of it as I can, in any way I please, before I make my
choices." After all, she said, as long as she didn't hurt anyone else, what she did was her own business. All those old
rules that Chaplain's generation had lived by were out.
And good riddance! They never did the world much good
anyway.

When someone in the group asked Joan during one of
those sessions what she was studying, she said that was one
of the open fields she was still roaming, but that she was
"toying with the idea" of psychology or anthropology.
"People interest me," she said, and wrapped up that topic
with a wonderfully engaging smile. She seemed far more
interested in sounding Chaplain out, or in challenging
him—with all her contradictions, Chaplain wasn't sure
which at first—about the new life-styles, the "—er—new

things going on, the experiments in human relations," she stammered just a little when she brought the topic up for general discussion the first time.

What was the matter anyway, she wanted to know, with "living with some guy, if that's what I want, or even with another woman? If that's what I want and it makes me happy and I'm hurting nobody, why not? If I want to have a baby without comitting myself to some fellow, why not? Let your conscience be your guide. It's no one else's business."

"Conscience?" Chaplain asked. "What does 'conscience' mean then when you use it like that?" He wasn't baiting her, but it was a major point and he did want to draw her out.

"It means," Joan answered in her most serious tone, "that if my conscience says it's all right to do something then it's all right. I'm the highest court of appeal for what I do."

There was no doubt that Chaplain was a match for Joan on the subject of "the new things going on." But he didn't know whether he could get through to her in any way that would make a real difference in this crucial matter of conscience, really answer that question "Why not?" so that she would be willing to see. That clash of opposites made such a racket in her soul, he didn't think she could hear him. Not really. And for all her agreeably tough and flippant ways, she seemed to be hiding. Her directness seemed a disguise for something she couldn't or didn't want to say. Her seemingly open manner was like a veneer that was designed, as veneers are, to be attractive and protective at the same time. All of those things were just some of the opposites clashing and banging away inside her.

Still, Chaplain had to try to get through to her, and pray for the best.

In the first place, he told her, these ideas she thought of as new and outrageous were really old and worn-out. He told her, told all who were gathered there, story after story, weaving them into a brief, heady history of "new life-styles" and "experiments" in living, from pre-Christian Athens and twelfth-century Constantinople and fifteenth-century London and eighteenth-century Boston. Except for some funny-sounding names, those stories appeared a lot like what Joan and Chaplain and his other evening visitors could see all around them, right now. Most of Chaplain's stories did not have happy endings. "If happiness is what you're after—" Chaplain smiled a craggy smile at Joan C., and left the rest unfinished. His old eyes, so experienced at pulling aside the curtains of pretense, seemed to fix her own eyes for one little moment, coaxing her to look past those curtains, too. But, no, he could see there was no response. Not yet.

Often, in a natural sort of way, Joan's problems or someone else's or an issue that sparked an evening's talk would be presented to Chaplain with the straight-out request that he talk about it. They liked thinking things through, but one of the enjoyable treats about coming here, especially in these years, was that Chaplain was a kind of guide for them, whatever their beliefs might be. This was one place where they didn't have to do all their thinking all by themselves, didn't have to "re-invent every wheel in the works," as one engineering student phrased it. They loved to hear him draw meanings they had never thought of from familiar Gospel stories. They were delighted with the color and the detail he was able to summon from a host of other sources he knew so well and that they had never discovered before.

Of course, Chaplain loved all that, too. Not just because he felt he was in his true home when he talked so intimately of Jesus and his life and his teaching. But because so many of these young people had never had a guide before, no one who talked about the reasons behind what people called right and wrong but merely expressed as rules. Joan and others like her were wrong to think that conscience was some personal, unassailable high court, Chaplain said. Conscience is love's barometer, and it is love's property. It was in these easy conversations that he had the opportunity to help form and guide the consciences of these young men and women, lightly, without beating them down or thumping his breast, but by showing with his stories of Jesus and his Apostles a little of what Jesus has shown us all.

But even in those conversations, Joan seemed to want to be the challenger. She seemed to want to hear Chaplain, but not to be pinned down by what she heard. That clash of opposites again! She was like a child in a rose patch, Chaplain thought, who loved the beauty and the fragrance, but who would run before she could be stung by a bee or caught by a thorn.

"Thomas!" Joan was quick to give her opinion in one of those sessions. "That's the Apostle for me! He knew how to ask hard questions!"

"That's a surprise, Joan," Chaplain wanted to take up the challenge. "I'd have guessed John would be your favorite. You have more in common with him, I expect, than you might be able to guess."

Joan's dark eyes flashed for a second, but she let his counter-challenge go by her, and Chaplain was disappointed.

"Almost," he thought. "She almost came out from behind the veneer, the pretense."

Well, he would just have to keep on trying. He wouldn't push too hard, of course, because he didn't want to drive her away. But he knew that the one honest thing Joan had said was that people interested her. And he knew it was not an academic interest, that it would never be quenched by courses in psychology and anthropology. What she called "roaming the fields of life" was, Chaplain understood, more in the nature of a search for someone to love her and a fear that no one would, or that she might miss some chance if she tarried too long. That was the deepest clash of opposites in Joan. That search and that fear were harder to deal with when there were no rules and no guidelines—no conscience, in fact. That was what made Joan both bold and timid. Chaplain was certain of that much. She would experiment with almost anything, and justify it the best way she could, with her "why-nots" and her "roaming the fields before she made her choices." There would be nothing to hold her back, he feared, from running and switching and experimenting and trying almost anything, like a blind woman begging everywhere for coins, who couldn't see that her purse was torn.

Unfortunately, Joan ran from Chaplain's rose patch as readily as from any other. After a few months of her challenges to Chaplain, and of her shying from even his gentlest counter-challenges, from his every effort to draw aside with her those curtains of pretense, she began to show up only rarely. And, finally, not at all.

She was missed more than she might have been able to see through those obstructive curtains. For, had she only known, she had found a little taste of what she was searching for. It wasn't only Chaplain, but others she met there, who cared about her, about the fields she might roam, about the choices she would make, the reasons she would give, and the fruits she would taste.

Chaplain sent messages to Joan for a while—gentle invitations—through some of his young people who shared classes with her. She sent back no word and brought none. Then after a while, she began to skip her classes; so she didn't get the messages at all. Still, some news about her filtered back to Chaplain, and he made quiet inquiries. He learned only bare outlines of her life.

She had moved off campus. There was another girl for a while. Then a young man. There was an arrest for possession of "illegal substances." The arrest brought Joan's parents from out of state to the local police department. Charges were dropped, on Joan's promise to have nothing more to do with the drug scene, to report to the dean's office regularly, and to bring her attendance and her grade average up sharply. Joan earnestly agreed to do all of those things, and did none of them.

Though Chaplain only learned the barest facts of Joan's "experiments with the new life-styles," he probably knew more about them than she did, and he could fill in the details without evening being told. Too much of everything—easy sex, easy drugs, easy promises, easy answers. Energy dissipating itself into nothing, searching endlessly for something to replace it. Watching the rest of the world from a greater and greater, a lonelier and lonelier, distance.

Even when there was no word of her any longer, Chaplain thought of Joan a great deal. He prayed and talked with Jesus about her in the late-night hours. In the light of his own friendship with Jesus, he would wonder about the darkness in which Joan was so desperately trying to find her way. She had so little guidance, so little instruction, so few who could give her examples of love to follow or any taste of the joy and sweetness that love brings. "Help her, my sweet and loving Lord," he would often pray. "And as you choose the weak things of this world to accomplish your work, let me help her, too. If there is no one else to guide her, bring her back."

At just such a moment, when it was late and quiet and he was alone, sharing his day and everyone's problems with Jesus, the unwelcome jangle of his telephone startled him. It was one of the young students Joan had met at Chaplain's, a pre-med student who worked part-time nights at the city hospital. Joan C. had just been brought in, he told Chaplain. It looked like suicide, but they weren't sure.

"Pills and alcohol by the look of it. She's in a coma. I know how much you care about her." The young man seemed nearly in tears by the sound of his voice. "I thought you'd want to know."

"Will she live?" Chaplain asked.

"It's too soon to say, Chaplain. They're doing all they can. But you know how it is with these things . . ."

Even as he took in the bad news, Chaplain wondered if this was the way Jesus had brought Joan back, if this was the way his prayer was to be answered. It might appear a brutal answer from a loving Lord. But there were times, Chaplain sighed, when it seemed Jesus was left no choice but to grasp you by the scruff of the neck and drag you back from whatever precipice you might be tumbling over.

"I'll be there in twenty minutes," Chaplain said into the phone. "Stay with Joan if you can, till I get there."

He was out the door and on his way in seconds.

✺

"Why not?" That had been Joan C.'s most constant challenge to Chaplain. It was like a banner she carried high in her battle of contradictions, a coat of arms she carried into life, her generation's version of "my will be done."

"Why not?" Two simple words that call into question everything Jesus and all his holy people—all his friends— ever taught about life and the way we should live it. Two words that frame the question every Christian asks, or is asked, a dozen times a day.

Why not experiment with everything? Why not treat life, as Joan had said, as an open field, roaming over it as much as you like, in any way you please? Why not make any choice you want to, for as long or short a time as whim or passion dictates? Why not have drugs, sex of any sort, all the kicks, all the thrills and all the disappointments too, as Joan had decided to do, when she left Chaplain? Why not try all the things Chaplain had sketched in those stories of ancient Greece, and of the Middle Ages, all the experiments, all the mistakes of all the ages?

The fact of the matter, as far as Chaplain could see, was that "Why not?" wasn't a question at all, for Joan's generation or for any that had come before. It was a statement. "Why not?" meant "Go ahead!" It was a command, even. It was the "my will be done" of today. It only looked like a question.

If your conscience is no more than a trip wire of your emotions, a gauge of enjoyment, then "Why not?" means "Go ahead!" If "right" is what the crowd you're with at the moment says it is, and "wrong" can be changed to "right" by a quick show of hands or a popularity contest or a newspaper poll, then "Why not?" means "Go ahead!" If "as long as I hurt nobody" means Jesus is nobody, then "Why not?" means "Go ahead!"

Of course, that's a very damaging viewpoint. And it is deception. It is a little like reading a sign on a crowded highway that says "Slow—dangerous curve ahead," and acting as though it means "Resume full speed." Only, when the signs you misread say "right" and "wrong" and "conscience," and when the road you're traveling on is the one-way road of your life of friendship with, or separation from, Jesus and everything he offers, then deception becomes a huge and terrible lie. If you miss his signs, his meaning, his love, then everything—all the "signs" we live by—mean crazy things that unravel in your hands.

Love means sex, and sex means experiment, and experiment means no commitments, and no commitments means no love. It all unravels. And then no love means loneliness, and loneliness means desperation, and desperation—well, desperation can mean almost anything. It can even mean Joan C. being rushed to a hospital, so that her stomach can be pumped, and caring people can try to save her life. It all unravels.

Those were just some of the things that Chaplain had hoped Joan would find out, before it all could start to unravel for her. That was why he was disappointed when she left, and when she ignored his little messages inviting her back, making her welcome. Those invitations weren't his alone. They were invitations of Jesus, extended through a friend. For that's how Jesus does things. "I have chosen you," the invitation always says in one way or another.

The problem seems to be that many people find it unbelievable that Jesus would choose us, would want to be with us, want to share everything we do, want to be present to us and have us present to him, really, intimately, even in the seemingly silly details of our individual lives. And yet, that is precisely what Jesus wants from each one of us.

As Chaplain sat through the night by Joan's bed, he prayed in that certain knowledge. Joan's pretty eyes were closed now, and sunken, and the obstinate mouth was slack. The unruly curls tangled on the pillow. But in his mind's eye, Chaplain saw again the quick passage of her moods across her face—fear, resentment, fight, a glimmer of hope. And he imagined with his soul's eye that she was roaming different fields now, fields between life and death, where, ready or not, she would have to make a choice—possibly, her final one—very soon.

How Chaplain wished he could talk to her, wished she could hear him. Almost tantalizingly, without his summoning the memory, he thought of some old movie—*Blithe Spirit* or *Topper* or one of those films that made death such a jolly affair. But at this moment he envied the film one advantage: By a photographer's trick, the audience had seen a dying woman's translucent image rise, leaving the solid form of her body slumped behind her. He wished he could find such a trick now, so that he could summon Joan's spirit to see with him what love and friendship with Jesus really mean; some way he could show her, before she made that final choice, what apparently no one had bothered or been able ever to show her in her whole life: the answer to all of her "why-nots."

He remembered how she had once announced the name of her favorite Apostle: "Thomas!" Her voice had been full of life and belligerence. "He knew how to ask hard questions!"

"John," Chaplain whispered again the name he had suggested before. "You have more in common with John than you might be able to guess."

He bowed his head then, his eyes closed, his forehead resting on the metal guardrail of the bed; and he laid his problem before his friend and beloved savior, Jesus.

❋

"Who put out the lights?," Joan tried to say, but her mouth felt thick and fuzzy and she wasn't sure anyone was there to hear her.

Where was she anyway? There was a dim pool of light spilling over a too-white bedspread, but she could only see a couple of yards or so. She could make out an i.v. bottle hanging above the bed where she lay. Everything else was in shadows. A hospital? Was she in some hospital? What was going on?

"Who put out the lights?" Joan tried again. "And where am I anyway? What's going on?"

She saw someone in a dark suit sitting in her little pool of light. If this was a hospital, maybe that was the doctor. But then she saw the craggy face and those eyes.

"Chaplain! What are you doing here? Can you tell me what's going on? Where am I?"

The craggy old face smiled in delight to hear that belligerent voice again, the stream of challenging questions. When he answered, he didn't pull any punches. "You're in the city hospital, that's where you are. You tried to run away from those fields you were so busily exploring. Suicide, they told me."

Joan thought for a moment. She remembered vaguely. Pills. A lot of pills. And alcohol. Just to be sure. She looked at Chaplain again. "You mean 'attempted suicide.' Here I am talking to you; so I must have botched it, right?"

"Maybe," Chaplain said. "The doctors say it's still too close to call."

Joan looked annoyed. This wasn't making sense to her, and she didn't like things that didn't make sense. "You mean I'm still unconscious? You're my dream or something? That's crazy!"

"If you think that's crazy," Chaplain mimicked Joan's impatient tone, but with an edge of tenderness, "just wait! And as to whether you're conscious or not, don't worry about it. You're awake in every sense that matters right now."

Chaplain turned partially away from Joan for a minute, and gestured to someone waiting in the darkness behind him. That must be the doctor, she thought, seeing the gown and all, as the newcomer stepped to the edge of her little circle of light. Now she'd find out what was going on! But it was a pretty funny gown for a doctor, brown and flowing right down to his ankles.

Joan's hopes faded. Probably just one of the crazy "friends" Chaplain liked to talk about during those sessions of his. One of those Apostles, or something.

No sooner had that thought come so easily into her head than she knew she was right. It was absolutely impossible, but she was absolutely right! She knew it!

In her amazement, she sat bolt upright in bed, only to find more surprises. She seemed to leave a part of herself, her flesh and bones, lying back there on the pillows and attached to those tubes from the i.v. "It must be the drugs," she glanced at Chaplain. "The whole thing must be the drugs."

"No," Chaplain smiled happily. "More like the answer to a prayer. My friend here—"

"Wait!" Joan held up her hand. Always belligerent! "Let me guess!"

With huge interest and no embarrassment at all, Joan studied the robed figure from head to toe. He was young, clean-shaven, his long hair was gathered at the nape of his neck with a colored kerchief. She didn't bother about the details of his clothes. It was his face and, above all, his eyes and the look in them that held her. She knew that look. She had been searching for it all her life. She always knew she'd recognize it when she saw it. It was the fullness and satisfaction and peace of someone who loved and was loved.

"John!" She smiled in triumph. "John, the beloved disciple! Am I right?"

"Yes, you're right." John smiled back, and glanced for a second at Chaplain. "You're just the kind of person Chaplain told us you were. But that's not a surprise."

"Yes, well," Joan was composed enough to make one of the little jokes she liked to hide behind, "you're the way Chaplain told us you'd be, too. And that is a surprise!"

"Is it?" John seemed interested more than amused.

Maybe apostles didn't have a sense of humor, Joan thought. She didn't want to offend him. Maybe she'd better explain.

"I mean," she explained, "here we are just about into the next century and sending messages to this star and that star, and rockets all over the place, and, well, you're not exactly E.T., you know. Who would expect some old clergyman to reach back two thousand years and make all those old stories he tells come true?"

"All those old stories he tells are true." John pulled up another chair, and he and Chaplain made themselves comfortable. "In fact, from what I can tell, you and I have a lot of very true, very real things in common."

Joan laughed a very unconvinced laugh. "So Chaplain said."

"Did you ask him why?" John wanted to know. "Did you hear him out?"

Joan had to admit she hadn't, and she smiled a little apology at Chaplain. Anyway, she thought, nothing lost! She was pretty sure John was going to explain all that now; that, that was why Chaplain had brought him here.

Nevertheless, John would have to be a pretty good talker to convince Joan that there was much common ground between them. She said so, straight out, just as Chaplain had told John to expect. Joan hadn't walked with God, with Jesus, she said, not even with holy men, except for those few months when she'd visited Chaplain. People nowadays were too busy for all that. There just wasn't time. And John had never had all these distractions, so many things going on, so much to try, so much that might just pass you by. Joan would listen, she said, but she'd be hard to convince.

For the moment, John chose not to answer what Joan said about walking with God. He preferred to begin at a point Joan would more easily recognize. He told her that, compared to what he had seen when he was her age—the age at which he stood before her now, give or take three or four years—Joan didn't know what distractions were! Chaplain could have told her a lot of it, if she'd had the patience to listen. "A lot is known about me, really," he smiled confidentially at her, "if you just know where to look it up, or listen to someone who does—like Chaplain.

"I wasn't always a fisherman. Oh, that was a good part of what my family did for a living, my father Zebedee and my elder brother James. I grew up a fisherman, in fact. But my mother, Mary, cocked an eye at grander things for me, and so did James, and I myself sometimes.

"Anyway, off I went with my family's blessing, south to Jerusalem, to present myself at the Temple and be educated as a priest.

"Now, I know that doesn't sound much like your going off to a university, but you can't imagine Jerusalem in those days. Jerusalem was already thousands of years old and very practiced in the ways of amusement. From the bawdiest to the most urbane; it was all there for the taking."

Joan shook her head and interrupted. "But you were going to be a priest. That's different . . ."

"Is it?" John was just as insistent as his impatient new friend. "Perhaps. But it was all offered to me, just the same. During my time there, I came into favor with the man who was serving the Temple as high priest just then. Annas was his name, father-in-law of a man called Caiaphas—you probably have heard about him. Just a few

years later, he was high priest himself and sat as Jesus'
judge. To be in the favor of men such as these, as I was,
was to have all doors open to you. All the doors of all the
families of power and means. All the doors of luxury and
diversion. All those fields that you went out to discover
and explore were simply opened up to me. If you remember such details of the Gospel, you'll recall that when I
went back there, three years later, I was still remembered
and still allowed free access to those rich houses."

John had been right to start his story with these little-
known facts of his life. Joan could see the similarity between the sort of place Jerusalem was and the things
Jerusalem offered in John's time and the fields of open
choices she had been looking for. But what she couldn't
see, she said with a frown, was why he had left all that
behind to return to Galilee and become a fisherman like
his father and brother.

John told her why. The artificiality. The snobbery.
The conformity. The curious darkness that seemed to
come over him when he was close to all that for too long. It
was, he said, as though someone had thrown a heavy blan-
ket over his head and shut out the air and the light of clean
day. "I wanted to see the light that glances off the waters of
Galilee Lake; I wanted the clean hard world of a fisherman. But, most of all, I wanted to get back to the simple
people who loved me. Not people who thought I was handsome or intelligent. Love: that was what I wanted most."

Joan had to admit that was another strong similarity.
That's what she wanted, too. But, she said, all similarities
ended with the desire. She couldn't go home to some Galilee Lake. To some simple life. Her parents loved her, she
supposed, but they were busy with their own problems.

Anyway, people nowadays were supposed to go out on their own, search, learn, find love. "Everybody does it," she said, "I just don't seem to be very good at finding it."

"Neither was I."

"What?" Joan was startled. "You're the beloved disciple! Next to Jesus, you practically *mean* love!"

"No," John contradicted her. "Only Jesus *means* love. *Is* love. Everyone else *learns* love. I learned it. Your favorite, Thomas, learned it. My brother James, Peter and his brother, Andrew, all of us. We all learned it. And we weren't very quick to catch on, considering that the teacher we had was Love incarnate.

"In fact, in the beginning, it was really my own satisfaction I was after. Remember, for example, the story of the Samaritan town, and the authorities who refused to let us spend the night there?"

Joan thought she remembered vaguely. "Wasn't that the time you asked Jesus to destroy the place with thunder and lightning?"

"That was the time," John confirmed. "Can you imagine? He was teaching us love. And we wanted to teach the Samaritans a much different lesson. We didn't think much of Samaritans anyway! And we also wanted Jesus to avenge our own pride. So we asked Jesus to draw on his divine power to kill those men with their wives and children where they stood!

"Jesus told us we didn't know what we were saying. And he was exactly right. He told us that he had come 'so that people may have life and have it more abundantly,' and not that they should perish on account of our hurt pride.

"He gave James and me a nickname that day, so that we wouldn't forget the lesson. 'The sons of thunder,' he called us.

"Well, we didn't forget that day, but we hadn't really learned the lesson. The real lesson, I mean. The lesson of friendship with Jesus. That lesson took us three years to learn. And more after that as well."

Joan's face took on that challenging look Chaplain had seen so often. "Well, then, I'm not so badly off. I mean. I never asked for thunder and lightning, for revenge. I was just looking for love. Honestly!"

"No," John contradicted her with a gentleness that made his meaning all the sharper. "No, not honestly. And that's the point. You've always told yourself you were looking for love. But you ran from it, the way you ran from Chaplain. You haven't tried to learn love. You've tried to find pleasure. For you, friendship has always meant doing what you thought would be pleasurable with other people. That's not the measure of friendship. And it's not the measure of love.

"Do you think Jesus suffered death on a cross for pleasure? He certainly suffered it for love's sake, though."

That question seemed to shock Joan. No, of course, she didn't think that, but . . .

"No, Joan. No buts. Let me tell you something about how friendship works. How it works when you walk by Jesus' side, as we did.

"In fact, let's start with that point. We were with him. Every day, whatever we were doing, we were with him. But most of the time it wasn't pleasurable, not in the way you mean when you 'look for pleasure.' That wasn't even the point of what we were doing. We were a working group. Jesus was preaching, teaching, curing, consoling. We were always on the move. Always about the work of Jesus, as Jesus was always about his Father's work. If we were at a feast or a banquet, it wasn't to carouse, it was to work. We slept in the open air. We gave up family and home and friends. We did all the things one would think would be a punishment. But everything we did, we did with him, and because of him. That was what made everything we did, the hard and the easy, different.

"And by the mere fact of being in the company of Jesus, of being with him, we began to learn suddenly a whole range of new things in the most intimate way—in a way we could not have learned apart from him. To be in his very presence was to understand deeply, suddenly, completely, that certain actions, certain behavior, certain thoughts and certain desires, created a distance between you and him, and so those things were not pleasurable. In fact they were painful. It was as though they did some violence to the love and the closeness between us. As though some curtain would be drawn between us. And we were the ones who had had the choice of drawing it open or closing it more and more. By what we did or did not do, I mean.

"Not huge things like wanting to call down the thunder of vengeance on the Samaritans. Even simple things. For example, we couldn't, simply couldn't, use even the everyday curse words that men used—especially men in boats. Remember, we were fishermen, used to fishermen's language. But in Jesus' presence we knew, by that quick interplay of human feeling, that we couldn't coarsen our lives even that much without placing a distance between ourselves and him, without opposing him in some way, opposing his love, his desire for us.

"Or take another example. Say, the behavior of men toward women. Any tendency to look at a woman and admire her in a merely sexual way—anything along that line was out! We knew it. Instinctively. And if there was anyone there—there wasn't to my knowledge—but if there was anyone among his Apostles and disciples who had any sort of homosexual tendency, well, that too was out. And we all knew it. Automatically.

"Now the curious thing was that all that sort of behavior was out when you were with him, not because he laid down a series of dos and don'ts. To be sure, he did talk about all those things to many people, and they thronged to hear him. They needed to hear all that. And so did we. But what really made everything he said, everything I'm telling you now, urgent and clear, was the one simple act of being with him. His very presence made those choices impossible, unless you wanted to draw that curtain—that distance—between yourself and his friendship.

"I didn't understand why then. But I did later. It was because he was and is Holiness itself, was and is God. Anything unholy, even in tendency and impulse, was as clearly felt as the sharpest pain from a physical wound. Only, in this case, we're talking about a wound to love. And a wound that removes you from love.

"Now, whether you've learned this yet or not, that's the way all friendship works, the way love works, the way human company works. Your very presence has a wordless influence on the person you're with."

"Wait!" Joan objected. "Wait! That may be the way it

worked for you. And for all the others back then. But you were *with* Jesus. I'll grant you, his influence worked like that. But you can see for yourself what happened to me." She gestured toward her unconscious body and the i.v. bottle dripping liquid into her veins. "Not everybody feels those wonderful influences you talk about."

John nodded. "I know," he said. "As I told you, we had to change; we had to learn. Our language, our behavior, all of it changed, because we wanted so much to be in the light of that love Jesus had, that Jesus was. But not everyone changed."

"What then?" Joan asked. "What if they didn't change?" She wanted to weigh the possibilities on her scale of "why nots."

"Well," John took up the other side of the question. "What happened to those who failed Jesus was that they couldn't stay in his company. They couldn't have it both ways. To stay would have meant they'd have had to change. Why? It's like asking why red can't be blue. It can't, without changing, without reflecting a different light. That's why the Rich Young Man went away sorrowfully. He couldn't reflect that different light, even for the sake of the love Jesus obviously had for him."

Chaplain could see that John was making progress, that Joan was struggling to understand. She had come out from behind that veneer, and she was really trying. Of course, John saw it too. And he leaned forward, to emphasize the point that was so essential for Joan now.

"That was what happened to Judas. He hung on and on, hoping to reach his worldly goals through Jesus. We had worldly goals too, the lot of us. But the difference was that we changed. Judas didn't. He finally had to make a choice. And he did. He contacted the enemies of Jesus. He had to leave the presence of Jesus in that most real sense of going over to Jesus' enemies. But the hatefulness of his particular sin—the first thing that strikes everyone about it—was that he came back and masqueraded as a friend, as a loving follower of Jesus. That was the very essence of his treachery. Pretended friendship. Deceit. His friendship was a lie. 'You betray me with a kiss,' Jesus said to Judas. Think about that, Joan! Those aren't just dramatic words. Judas used the most intimate and sacred and universal sign of love for its very betrayal, for its very opposite. He was with Jesus, but he wasn't with him really—like a lot of people who act as if they were Christians but aren't really.

"Those of us who were really with him, really absorbed in him—because we loved him—were necessarily molded and changed by his very presence. It became deeply painful for us to do anything that would separate us from him even a little bit. That's one of the things that love does.

"Of course, there were certain central and key lessons he gave us. Be like little children, he said. A simple lesson? Oh, yes. But it is a key to understanding. A child, weak and small as it is, must trust. And unformed as it is, it must learn love and learn what love demands. It must learn what will bring it close to love, to love's friendship, and what will separate it from all of that. Instinctively, a child puts out his arms to be taken up. Instinctively, it asks for love. It must learn how to grow in the love it needs so much, and on which its life depends.

"Joan, *we* had to learn all of that, as you also have to learn it. Be like little children, he said. Trust love, he was saying. Learn everything in love, he was saying. Trust me. Learn everything in me. Love me. I am Love itself.

"But there was always the other side of the coin. You were right," he smiled at Joan. "Not everybody feels those wonderful influences I've been telling you were so freely showered on us. Jesus was not the only teacher in this world, and that is as true now as it has been always.

"That was the point of another basic lesson he gave us. Beware of the Father of Lies, he told us. For if you look back, look back at all your wild days, didn't your behavior revolve around lies and deceptions and traps for other people? And others' for you?

"When you told someone you loved them, most of the time what you really were saying was, 'Let me use you for my pleasure,' wasn't it?

"And when you said, 'Oh, my conscience tells me it's okay to get stoned on heroin, or take such and such a partner,' wasn't that a lie? What really happened was the other way around. Your desire said Get stoned! Take that person as a sexual partner! And then you wiped out that word desire, and replaced it with the magic word conscience. You said, 'My conscience says it's okay.' Whatever you wanted to do, you simply trained yourself to say a certain progression of things, as though reciting a magic formula: 'I feel like doing it; therefore I shall do it; therefore my conscience says, "Do it!"' If you reflect a little, you'll admit that much."

"*My* conscience," Joan interrupted, "said, 'Why not?'"

John smiled. "Still, it was your magic formula to live your life by, but in which everything is backwards. Just as Chaplain here says all the time. You get it backwards, and you live it backwards; and everything you do comes out backwards.

"Why? Because in Jesus' presence you can't live a lie!

Or, if you try, then you will find you have left his presence. You may blink in your surprise at being so far away, in fact; and you may blame it on him. But the simple truth, however unfashionable it is—but then, simple truth has nothing to do with fashion; it simply is what it is forever— the simple truth is that every lie, every deceit, every backwards twist makes you resemble the Father of Lies, Satan. And between Jesus and Satan there is unending war, unending hate.

"That was what we learned about love and friendship on this earth, those of us who walked with Jesus. We came to see that in all we did and all we thought, we were either closer to Jesus, who *is* Love, or we were farther from him. Our thoughts, our actions, took on meaning, gave us a deeper pleasure, a deeper reward, than we had ever imagined, because we did them for him, because of him.

"It wasn't a question of, 'I feel like doing something,' and 'because I feel like it, I will do it.' It wasn't a question ever of 'why not?' It was a question of testing every act, every thought in the love we had for Jesus, in his approval, just as the children he told us to imitate seek the approval of their fathers and mothers who love them and teach them love.

"When Christians talk about conscience, about developing conscience, that's what they mean. Chaplain calls it learning what it is in you that makes possible or impossible the love of Jesus."

If anyone had ever seen revelation begin to dawn in the eyes of a human being, John and Chaplain saw it in Joan's eyes at that moment. Love. Learning. Conscience. Trust. Jesus. They had all been words made up of little letters, not words that opened doors to a universe of truth.

But there was something new for Joan now. She was at the very threshold of wanting what John was offering, clearly offering. But she wasn't sure. She was just wavering.

"Yes," she nodded her head. Then, "No," she contradicted herself. That bundle of contradictions hadn't been sorted out. Not quite yet. "What I mean is, you said yourself, you were with him, with Jesus, with God. It was easier for you. Oh, I know. You said it was hard sometimes. And I know what you said about pleasure. I don't mean that. I mean, you actually could see him and touch him. You rested your head on his shoulder. It was easier . . ."

"Was it?" John's question was a prod. "He wasn't always with us. We all lived here after he had gone. I lived longest of all. Yet, as you say, I am remembered as the beloved disciple, as the one who wrote the deepest things about love."

"But you had the memory, the real memory."

For the first time, John raised his voice. "The *memory*! Joan, do you think Peter died upside down on a cross for a *memory*?

"Do you think my own brother, James, who dreamed once of glory, was depending on a *memory* when they took him to one of the highest walls of old Jerusalem and threw him down on to the rocks below? A *memory*?

"And for all the long decades I spent in Ephesus surrounded by enemies, immersed in poverty, do you think it was a *memory* that sustained me?

"And what about all the ones who came after us? Even Paul. And *all* the martyrs, *all* the holy people who never even met Jesus, yet renounced worldly pleasures, suffered what no *memory* would ever induce them, or enable them, to endure?

"No! Not a *memory*. He *was* with us, *is* with you, every moment.

"And you, Joan, you and every single person you have ever seen, has an advantage even *we* didn't have in the days we walked this earth with him. We only knew that we loved him and never wanted to be parted from him. Only that.

"It was only later, after Jesus had died and was risen from the dead, and ascended to the Father in Heaven, that we could really begin to understand what you can understand right now, without waiting, as we had to wait, fearful, disappointed, in that upper room. It was only then, when Jesus sent the Holy Spirit, just as he had promised, that we had the same grace at our disposal as you have had ever since you were baptized!"

Joan was trying, really trying to follow. Another step, just one more step. "Grace? What grace? What's that got to do with Jesus' own presence?"

"Everything. Everything! Jesus is—or can be, wants to be—present to you in your heart and soul now in a way that he was not present to us until he left us. You can literally do everything in his presence, because he can be present with you in all things—if, the big if!—if you decide to cultivate his company, accept his friendship, allow love of him to modify your life. Just as it was when he was here among us as a man, just as it was when he sent his Spirit. He has already entered your company. He will not change. *You* must. He has accepted you. You must accept him. *You've* got to enter *his* company."

"Enter his—" It was only a whisper from Joan, as gentle as the change by which she began to repeat John's words, not in order to examine them this time in the scale of her "why nots," but to savor them, like morsels offered to her parched and starving soul. This must be grace. This must be what John meant by grace.

It was so quiet and tranquil, so undisturbing, so gentle. For one brief moment, the invisible hand of Jesus touched her soul. She saw. She understood. Immediately. Without shock. Without a sudden tremor. Only the grace of Jesus could do that. It was the invitation to her soul that only Jesus could offer. There were no words now, no pictures in her imagination, no thoughts in her mind. But there was a great, profound, sudden access to peace when everything in her, her very being, looked around for the first time to discover that Jesus had been there all the time, that he had never been absent, had never left her. She was allowed by that grace of Jesus to enter his presence for those precious moments, to be among the holy ones around him, among the saints and his chosen ones who are always in his presence and therefore are holy with his holiness.

All her shabbiness fell away like a worn-out, irritating piece of clothing, like shoes that had pinched and blistered her feet. She was free in herself. She breathed the fresh air of his presence. Her lies, her self-deception, her desire to consume her energies in the surfeit of her senses, all that was suddenly removed. And her first instinct was the same as it always was and always is when Jesus' grace touches the human soul, the same as it was with the man in the Gospel who asked humbly: "Lord, what must I do in order that I have the eternal life that you promise?"

"How do I—What must I—" She stumbled, groping for words she was unaccustomed to using.

Chaplain, eyes brimming with tears, looked at John,

for whose presence and help he had so earnestly prayed. Chaplain knew what the sweetness of that moment was for Joan C. And he knew that, if she did not accept it now, the moment would pass, and might never return. He knew that, in a certain true sense, all of Heaven and all of Hell hung suspended, focused from eternity, from forever to forever, on this place, on this instant of time, on this little mortal, this belligerent, beloved fugitive from the battle of "Why not?" lying in a drug ward of a public hospital, testing for her soul's sake Jesus' sacrifice on the cross. Could he save this one small soul? At the moment's end, would all of Heaven be able, in Jesus' words, "to rejoice at the conversion of one sinner?" Or would the Enemy triumph?

God himself, the great God of the ages, and of the universe, bent down with all of Heaven, awaiting her answer.

"Who put out the lights?"

It was just a whisper, but it was enough to wake Chaplain. He must have dozed off as he was praying. He raised his head from the metal guardrail of the bed and looked anxiously at Joan's face, so white and drawn in the dim pool of light. Was she awake? Her eyes seemed to flutter open for a second. Had she spoken? Was she coming out of it?

"Who put out the lights? Where am I anyway? What's going on?" Just a whisper. But at least that!

"You're in the city hospital," Chaplain answered. He had the feeling that he was replaying a memory. Bits of his dream came back to him—John in the brown, flowing robe, sitting with him here by Joan's bed. He shook off the memory, gave his full attention to Joan. "You're in the city hospital," he said again. "We weren't sure you were going to make it."

Joan turned her head weakly to see who was talking to her. "Chaplain?" she whispered. "Funny, I just had a dream about you. And," she knitted her brows in groggy confusion, opening and closing her mouth, feeling the dryness, "and . . . John, I think it was John . . ."

She seemed to drift off again. Chaplain was startled. *Joan* had a dream about John?

He would have to puzzle that out later. Now he had to get the doctor, let him know Joan was conscious, appeared to have made her choice to live.

When all the medical bustling had quieted down again, and Chaplain was sure she needed nothing more for the moment, he prepared to leave. Joan was still groggy. She slipped in and out of sleep. She asked him to call her parents, to tell them she was sorry, and that she loved them, and not to worry. Chaplain promised he would, though he expected they were on their way here, and she could say all that to them herself.

"Chaplain . . . ?"

He turned back to her bed.

"Chaplain. About John. I had this dream. Or something. Do you believe in dreams? It was about John, you know—John? The Apostle? And about the 'why nots' of life. And conscience. You were in it, too. It was so peaceful. That was when I woke up. Chaplain, will you come back and see me? I mean, today? Please? Later today? I—I need to ask you some questions. I really need some help."

"Orrite, Joan." Chaplain could hardly believe his ears.

"I'll be back. Later today. And we'll talk." At last, he thought, we'll really talk.

"Yes . . ." Joan drifted off into sleep again.

Chaplain raised his eyes brimming with real tears this time. "My Lord Jesus, whose dream was that anyway?"

In Chaplain's peaceful soul, his good friend, Jesus, answered him: "Mine!"

The Betrayal
of the Lovely Family

BETRAYAL OF LOVE AND LOVE'S

RESPONSE

M*ATTHEW!*"

In forty years, no one on Ed D.'s staff could remember hearing him bellow like that, much less remember seeing his face go beet-red with anger. But there it was! His eyes blazed. And the way he strode full tilt past the desks into his office, why, anyone would have thought he was a man of thirty-five! Heads turned to watch. Hands covered ears as he slammed the door shut behind him with all the energy of his fury. Then, in the stunned quiet he left behind, heads whispered together at those desks.

"Matthew?" they buzzed. "Why would he shout for old Mr. Matthew who's been dead and gone for the past ten years!"

"Matthew Lovely!" Wide-eyed, they heard the shout again from behind that closed door.

Ed D. stood shaking, staring in his anger at the gilt-framed portrait of his father-in-law, the founder of Lovely's Retail Enterprises, Inc. Old Matthew's face smiled its calm oil-painted smile, eyes focused, as always, on the opposite wall of the office, the wall right behind Ed's chair.

"Matthew! You look at me! That Judson! Your grandson! He's no Lovely! Not even as much as I am, and I only married into the family. You mark my words, Matt. That Judson is a Judas! That's what he is!"

Ed slumped a little as his anger drained his energy. He suddenly felt his age.

"Judas!" Ed D. muttered again, and turned away from Matthew Lovely's face for a moment. He moved over to his desk and sat down in his chair.

Ten years since Matt died, and Ed still missed the talks they used to have, the plans they used to make together. It gave Ed a sense of continuity to have that portrait in his office; and, though most of the time he didn't actually talk to it—he wasn't crazy, after all—that painting did always remind him of the vivid reality of the goals and the dreams and the values that had always been important to Matt, the things that still were important as far as Ed was concerned.

Say what you like, those were the very things that Ed knew had made Lovely's what it had become: the envy of the retailing world, the chain with one of the most satisfactory balance-sheets going, the little store that had become a legend, a national success story, a great retailer with branches in twenty-one states—and yet, still a place where people felt good about going to work or going to buy. Over half a century after its ragtag beginnings, and for all of its hundreds of millions of dollars in sales every year, and its thousands of employees, Lovely's was, in its entirety, as close to a big "family" as ever a business could become.

At least, that's the way it had been. Judson's plots and schemings would change all of that. Ed gave it six months. No more. Judson K., Matthew Lovely's only grandson, Ed's only nephew, the only Judas in the Lovely family. But one is all it takes.

Outwardly, Ed was calmer now. But inside he was still deeply angry, immensely troubled and hurt. Ready to pack it in, in fact, was the way he was thinking. There was no way out of this trouble. Judson had the power to sell out. Matt had seen to that. And why not? His only grandson, and a wizard at numbers and finance. Who should Matt have trusted his business to, if not his own family? But Matt would turn over in his grave, if he knew how Judson had sold out that trust, betrayed everything Matt had believed in, all his long life. Those were Ed D.'s sad thoughts as he glanced up again at the smiling face in the gilt frame.

Matthew Lovely had been one of the legendary pioneers of modern American retailing. There were dozens of men like him once, not all that long ago. Men who started with a pushcart or a horse and dray, selling goods from door-to-door. Unlike a lot of those men, though, Matt Lovely was not here today and gone forever, once a sale was made. He stuck by his word and honored every bargain he ever made. It was a point of honor and pride with him, and "just plain good business," he used to say. But it was also one more thing. He had cared about people as people. "And customers are people, first," he used to say. So he guaranteed everything he sold, even back then, whether it was a spool of thread or a bolt of the best yard goods. Whatever it was, Matt's guarantee went with it.

Before very long, the bargains he made became bigger than threads and thimbles, and there were more and more of them. Still, Matt always kept his word and his customers always knew it. After a while, he had enough money and enough customers to open a tiny store. Instead of his tramping the streets for fourteen hours a day, people came to him. And, when more and more people came, he moved to a bigger store, and he hired more people to help him, and he went to school at night to learn accounting so he could be sure things would "remain as they should be," even though he was too busy by then to manage it all himself.

Being sure that things remained "as they should be" was very important to Matt, and that unusual kind of caring never changed through all his long life and all his legendary success. In fact, Ed believed, Matt's success came because of something that didn't seem to have anything to do with business at all—or at least, not directly.

The durability of Lovely's Retail, and the success of Matthew Lovely's dream, Ed was certain, came from Matt's honest belief that service and caring about people were more important than anything else. For Matt, caring and service were the implied and most basic pledges behind every life and every business, his and everyone else's.

"If you do well what you do for a living," Matt used to say in some of those long talks Ed missed so much, "and you treat people the way you know ninety-nine out of one hundred people want to be treated, with honest respect and caring, the rest will take care of itself. Oh, you can't go squandering pots of money on wasteful nonsense, don't get me wrong. But I'll tell you this, Ed," Matt would shake his head for emphasis, "the minute you put the bottom line at the top of the list of things that matter, that's the minute you'll start downhill. Because that's the minute you'll start caring less about what you do and less about the way you do it. It will seep into your whole life and your very soul."

When he had first heard that speech from Matthew Lovely, Ed D. was still a youngster, not much older than Matt had been when he started out tramping the streets with his wares. Ed was already a valued member of the Lovely Retail family—that's the way everyone thought about Lovely's, as a *family*. In time, Ed would meet Matt's oldest daughter, fall in love, marry. But in Ed's earliest days with Lovely's Retail that was all in the future. Back then, Ed was openly puzzled by Matthew Lovely's thinking.

"What's the matter with watching the bottom line?" he remembered asking. "That's what business is for, making money. Isn't it?" He could almost hear his own voice echoing back at him across all those years. And Matt's voice too.

"Oh," Matt Lovely had said, "you watch that profit line. Good idea! But what I said was, don't put the bottom line at the top of your list of important things. I'm not sure that poverty by itself means you are virtuous. But I am sure that the things of Heaven are more valuable than anything else. 'Love the things of Heaven and you shall have everything else besides.' The things of Heaven that I have at my disposal right here, every day, are caring and service. Whatever the Bible means by 'everything else besides' I'll just have to leave to the good Lord."

Except maybe for the Gideons, Ed had never heard of businessmen, especially successful ones like Matt Lovely, quoting Scripture and giving sermons in their offices. In

fact, Matt didn't talk like that to everyone—he was groom-
ing Ed to be a trusted partner, even then. But Matt did act
like that to everyone. Everything he did seemed to stem
from his belief in God and in the "the things of Heaven"
he had at his disposal.

And his philosophy didn't end with his customers.
Lovely's provided every benefit for its employees that any
union might have thought up—and more besides. There
were retirement benefits and hospital benefits and bonuses
and the kind of job security and job advancement that
come from a deep mutual understanding of the work to
be done and a commitment to do it well. There wasn't a
trace of "one-upmanship" or "hard sell." Employees
worked at Lovely's for the same reason customers bought
at Lovely's—because they truly felt the caring spirit, and
because that's where they truly wanted to be. Over the
years of growth and success, unionizers were as frustrated
as Lovely's retail competition: Anything they might think
of, Matt Lovely had already done, and he did it first because of that spirit of caring that came high above the
bottom line on his list of important things.

Matthew Lovely and his wife, Meg, had never been
blessed with sons. Their daughters had never been in-
clined to join their father's business, though Matt would
have liked that. And, of the men his daughters married, Ed
D. was the only one who was also part of the Lovely's
Retail family. Matt's first grandchild—his only grandson, as
it turned out—was Judson K., the son of his youngest
daughter, who lived a thousand or so miles away.

There were visits and letters and phone calls and
photos that marked the years as Judson went through
grade school, made his high school football team, was ac-

cepted at three of the best colleges in the country, took his graduate degree in business administration with honors. Matt was proud of everything his grandson did, wished he could have been closer to him in his growing-up years.

So it was no wonder that he was happier than Ed could ever remember on the day Judson accepted Matt's invitation to join Lovely's Retail.

"Can you beat it, Ed?" Matt had come smiling into Ed D.'s office. "With that business degree he could have gone anywhere—banking, Wall Street, anywhere. But he called this morning and accepted my offer! Can you beat it?"

Ed was almost as happy about Judson's decision as Matt was. Lovely's was going to continue as a real family affair after all. Matt was no youngster, and Ed wouldn't be around forever, either. Judson would be a visible guarantee to employees and customers alike, to everyone who valued what Lovely's was, that the special spirit that had always been the heart of Lovely's would continue, even if the world around it seemed to be changing at such a drastic rate.

When Judson K. walked in the front door of Lovely's flagship store as assistant treasurer and controller, it was by his own choice; and he had made that choice carefully. Coldly, some might have said if they could have seen inside his head. He had weighed his decision on the scales with all of his other possibilities. After all, he had been eagerly interviewed by scouts from major national companies who had visited his university. He had made some inquiries on his own. Handsome offers came his way, too, no doubt about that. But there was no doubt that Judson had done his homework well, and was aware in some detail of the remarkable empire his grandfather had built. There were three hundred or so stores of varying size spread over half the states in the Union, turning nearly three-quarters of a billion dollars in sales.

In the end, one thing was certain in Judson's mind. No other company he considered offered him more promise, more power, or more instant prestige. And into the bargain there was the undeniable fact that few companies had more potential still ahead of them than Lovely's Retail— with the right hand to guide it forward into lean, modern business practice.

Under Matt's personal guidance and with Ed D.'s constant and willing help, Judson learned everything about his grandfather's company that could be taught. He spent months with the most experienced staff, learning, buying, receiving, shipping, warehousing, merchandising, display, advertising, community relations. He spent more months traveling to Lovely branches across the country, learning the operations Matthew had set up and developed with that caring mind of his. And he was welcomed everywhere, right up to those planning meetings where his grandfather shared, with the men and women who were his most intimate colleagues, his philosophy and his plans and his concerns and his own deeply felt personal loyalty.

The first time Judson heard his grandfather quote Scripture in one of those executive meetings, he smiled. He wasn't surprised, as Ed had been years before. After all, Judson's mother was Matt's own daughter, and Judson had been brought up on all the family stories. He knew about his grandfather's spiritual values that were such an important beacon for everyone at Lovely's Retail. Still, everyone knew that Judson's specialty and his interest and his value to the Lovely family were on the business side of things. Judson felt he had no apologies to make for that.

As time passed, Judson was made full treasurer and vice-president, had two children of his own, became a prominent member of the community and a pillar of Matthew's own church.

Everyone, including Ed, thought it would just be a matter of time before Matt stepped down as president and chairman of the board of his great enterprise and gave full power to his grandson. And maybe that's what he intended to do. Not even Ed knew for sure. For Matt had died very suddenly and peacefully one night in his bed, never having changed the provisions he had made years before for Ed D. to become the head of Lovely's Retail.

Ed looked up at Matt's portrait again. "Did you know then," he wondered aloud, "what it's taken me ten years to learn? Did you know then what a wizard your grandson is with money and shares and debentures and the power that goes with them? Did you suspect then how he would quietly maneuver us all into decision after decision, slowly using the trust we all had in him to do just what you always warned against?"

Ed got up from his chair and paced his office slowly. He reconstructed in hindsight what he hadn't been smart enough to anticipate. He saw how Judson had maneuvered in meetings and consultations, recommending new management blood, better management techniques, ways to "get the whole operation moving in tune with the times." It made Ed's head spin and his blood boil to think how he'd been taken in. Why hadn't he seen it all coming?

Well, it didn't matter any more! Today's board meeting had been clear enough. Judson had taken his long and careful time about it. But the sum total of it all was that he had won Ed's and everyone else's confidence, and along with it all the power he needed to commit Lovely's Retail to a merger with a publicly owned company, one of the most cutthroat outfits that had ever come down the retail pike, an upstart newcomer that made fortunes for a few by buying up and then gutting first-line retail chains.

"Just think of it," Judson had told them all in that meeting, his eyes bright with excitement. "The bottom line will be fantastic!"

Ed had jumped to his feet. He had argued and he had refused his agreement as head of Lovely's. And when he had said all he had to say, Judson simply told him he had all the company equity he needed. Ed didn't doubt that. Judson was family, after all. And the relatively few holders of the private shares in Lovely's Retail had no reason not to trust Judson. The merger was a fact, legally binding and legally done.

Ed knew he was beaten. And he knew what to expect. Judson had been more than a match for Ed, and maybe he had even fooled Matt—though Ed wasn't so sure about that now. Maybe that was why Matt never had taken that final step of giving his blessing to Judson's sole leadership of Lovely's.

It was no comfort to Ed that Judson would get the same treatment as everyone else in this merger. Service and caring would be out the window in six months, tops. The Lovely name for excellence would be exploited. But the bottom line would be at the top of the list of important things. In fact, the bottom line would be the whole list.

Old employees would go, like it or not, and be cheated

out of benefits into the bargain. New faces, young bodies with sharp minds and sharper pencils would be everywhere, making their careers on the backs of everyone else, making new bottom-line rules, setting new bottom-line standards. And Judson would be shoved aside as shabbily as everyone else, whether he knew it now or not. It was all over. Everything Matt had believed in and worked for, everything Ed had spent his life to help build. It was all over. There would be no more planning, no more being sure things remained "as they should be," no more "loving the things of Heaven and leaving the rest to the Lord."

"I'm sorry, Matthew," Ed had tears brimming in his eyes when as he looked at that portrait again, tears for Judson as much as for every one of them. Matthew had had great hopes for Judson, had placed such possibilities in his hands. "Maybe if I'd been wiser . . ."

He walked over to the windows and looked out at the late afternoon traffic. How could it happen, he wondered. How can anyone account for such betrayal? Judson planned it so well. Dear God in Heaven! How can anyone survive such darkness of soul? How can Judson or any of us survive it?

"Judas!" Ed hissed again to the darkening sky.

❋

"Judas"—the name Ed called his own nephew—sums up the greatest horror and the greatest enigma for the Christian mind. That name is the very synonym for traitor. It is the name of the only person in all of human history about whom we know from the lips of Jesus himself, unequivocally, that he was condemned to Hell.

That we know he was condemned to Hell is the horror. The enigma is more complicated. And it lies in Judas himself.

By all accounts, Judas was an intelligent man. He was one of only twelve men whom Jesus picked out from among all the multitudes—from the thousands who flocked to be with Jesus, to hear him, to receive a crumb from the table of salvation—to be in his constant company. Judas was one of the twelve privileged to walk by the very side of Jesus for the best part of three years. He saw Jesus raise the dead to life, feed multitudes, cure the blind, cure lepers and the lame and the dying. He shared day-by-day the intimacy of meals, conversation, journeys with Jesus. He heard Jesus preach. He heard the parables, and then heard those parables explained by Jesus himself. How could he have had all that—how could he have heard and seen what all the prophets and all the kings and queens since Abraham had dreamed of, for those three years—and then, at the heel of the hunt, have betrayed Jesus for thirty silver coins? For anything?

Yet even that is not the whole enigma. Perhaps not even the greatest one. To my mind, the most awful questions about Judas are these two:

First, the plain fact is that to be in the company of Jesus, was to be in a school of love, *the* school of love. Everyone there was called personally by Jesus to be his beloved friend. "All the things my Father has revealed to me, I have told you," Jesus said to them more than once. Why did Judas, alone of all the twelve, not learn that most central lesson? Why did he alone of all the twelve choose not to be beloved of Jesus, or to love Jesus?

The second question is this: Even after so terrible a

betrayal, even if his sins were as scarlet as blood—in this case the innocent blood of Jesus—why could Judas not do what he had seen so many people do eagerly, joyfully? "Even if your sins are scarlet," God promises in the Bible, "I will wash them whiter than the driven snow." If strangers came in the simple, strong faith that Jesus could and would wash their most terrible sins from them, why not Judas, who knew that Jesus forgave, forgave everything and everyone—once they were willing to be forgiven? Jesus spent his entire life among men forgiving repentant sinners. "I have not come to call the righteous to salvation," he said. You couldn't have been with Jesus for long —certainly not for three years—without having noticed his overwhelming desire to forgive you, to embrace you, to take you back into his friendship and love. "Your sins are forgiven," he had said so many times, to so many people whom everyone else shunned, people who had done vile things. "Go now and sin no more." It was as simple as that. Even the centurion who would bind Jesus and take him to Pilate, even he received Jesus' compassion and healing when the ever impetuous Peter cut off his ear. Even the soldier who supervised the whole grisly execution of Jesus —who perhaps himself pounded those square-shanked spikes into his flesh in three places, and drove a lance through the heart of Jesus—even he repented. "In truth, this was a just man, the son of God," he said; and in Christian tradition he is renowned as a convert who later was baptized and died as a martyr for love of that Jesus whom he had crucified. Even he now belongs to Jesus forever.

It is clear enough that Judas repented of his betrayal of Jesus, at least in the sense that he was sorry Jesus would be killed. Why did Jesus not forgive him, save him? Was it, as we often think, because Judas' betrayal was so enormous, because Jesus, whom he betrayed, was God himself? Was it, as we often think, because the execution of Jesus, the direct result of that betrayal, was the cardinal event in all of human history, the event, in fact, on which the meaning of all human history hangs? Was it, in other words, that Judas' betrayal concerned the capital event in the history of our universe?

Or is there something even more that we need to think about? Something that, even as with love itself, involves each one of us, each day of our lives?

For just as surely as every act of love and friendship can only take place successfully in Jesus' prior love and his prior friendship, so every betrayal of love, of friendship, of caring, is a betrayal that reaches to Jesus himself. "When you do these things to any one of these, my least ones," Jesus was clear, "you do them to me."

What was it that removed Judson, like Judas, to such a distance from love and from love's trust that he could betray them so? Whether Ed D. realized it or not in so many words, these were the questions that lay behind the tears that brimmed in his eyes that bleak afternoon of Judson's betrayal.

Ed's tears were not all for Judson. Those who are caught in the effects of betrayal, even if they are not the intentional targets, cannot be left out of the reckoning. They are sorely tried. All they believe in, all they live by and for, is put to a hard test at the hands of the betrayer. What if they fail, too? Where is their help? "Who can survive it?"—that was Ed's anguished question.

That question and all the other questions he asked that day, and the ones that lay like writhing ghosts behind them, are fair questions. All Christians ask them at some time, in one way or another. And Jesus has answered them all, for all time, in one way or another.

❋

"*ED!*"

The call was sharp and clear, a friendly imitation of Ed's much angrier shout when he had stormed back to his office after that dismal board meeting. But Ed was so absorbed in his brooding he didn't seem to hear; it was as though he had entered another world. And perhaps he had.

"Ed!" The voice was more insistent. "You called me and I'm here. Now, either you give me a good, clear explanation for all that ranting and shouting, or I'll be on my way!"

Ed stirred at the window. There was no ignoring *that* command, or the familiar voice that gave it.

"Nonsense!" He shrugged his shoulders. It was only his own tired mind, playing tricks, playing with his unspoken wishes. For Ed did wish he could talk things over with old Matt just now.

"Ed, you stubborn donkey! Turn that hard head of yours around and look at me!"

If wishes were horses, beggars would ride—wasn't that the old saying? Well, if Ed's wish could take flesh, Matt would be standing behind him right this minute, dead and gone, or not—and he'd be getting very impatient.

It only occurred to Ed later that he had felt no fear at all, not a twinge of it, even from the first inkling that something very unusual was happening. In fact, he was never able to put into words how he had felt, except to say that words fail when the impossible happens. And that was about all he was able to say then, in that office.

"That's impossible!" It was an incredulous whisper, a hoarse acknowledgment as he turned from the window and saw Matt standing not ten feet from him in the late day's dimming light. He was there all right, though. Not a mere oil painting. Not a painted smile. He looked just the way he had the last time Ed had seen him, quick blue eyes, quick smile, even the same dark tweed suit. It was all real, no trick of his mind.

"Yes, I suppose it is impossible." Even Matt's voice was the same. And that same right-to-the-point directness Matt always had: "But that's not what we're here to talk about. I gather you think you have a crisis on your hands."

Another thing that only occurred to Ed later was the amazing ease with which he settled into the impossible, plunged into the conversation he had so wished he could have.

"Think I have a crisis? Matt, the whole enterprise, the whole dream, everything we built—Judson has sold it all, betrayed everyone! It's over! That's a *crisis!*"

Matt turned on one of the lamps in the large office, settled into a comfortable chair nearby, and gestured for Ed to do the same. Just like old times.

And just like old times, too, Ed sat down and in that quite impossible conversation, summed up for Matthew Lovely all the terrible truth about Judson K.'s betrayal. When he had finished, there was silence for some time. Finally, it was Matt who spoke again.

"Ed, I know there's a crisis. But the reason I came is to help you understand that the real crisis isn't what you think. The real crisis isn't that Lovely's Retail is going to change. It isn't even that the infamous bottom line is going to become the iron rule that dictates policy and decisions—"

"But, Matt," Ed jumped to his feet, "you were the one who always said that bottom line should never top the list of important things. And you were right!"

"I'm still right," Matt held up his hand in a calming gesture. "But isn't that what you're doing now, Ed? Putting the bottom line at the top of the list of important things?" He saw Ed's look of confusion, and answered it quickly. "Oh, not the way Judson has. He sold out for it. But now that he's done that, isn't the most important thing the betrayal? Or rather, what is to become of the betrayer and the betrayed?"

"But Lovely's Retail, Matt! What about that?"

"What about that, Ed, is that it can go its mortal way, like everything else on this Earth, and still leave the most important things alive and intact. Oh, don't get me wrong . . ."

Ed smiled. Matt had always used that expression, and it was wonderful to hear it from him again, a gentle touch reminding him of other days.

". . . don't get me wrong. Lovely's was important. Everything we did, everything everyone does, is important. Partly for the obvious reasons. I mean, we do have to earn our living while we're here, and we need some place to live, and we must care for our families and our friends. But each one of those situations that make up the circumstances and the events of our mortal lives is part of the whole spectrum in which we work out our salvation. You remember that old Christian phrase, Ed? 'Work out our salvation'?"

Ed nodded. Of course he remembered.

"Well, Ed, we were very fortunate to have had what we did as the—well, let me call it 'the arena'—in which to make our choices and do our work in a way we felt we could offer to God."

Ed still objected. "Maybe I'm just dense, Matt, but that's what I just said. That 'arena,' as you call it, our arena, Lovely's, is gone, down the chute, finished."

"Right!" Matt leaned forward, blue eyes on fire with his intent, fixing Ed's attention on his words, pulling him out of anger and self-pity, inviting him to see something different. "That arena is gone. But it already has been replaced by another one. Instantly, immediately replaced. That's what I want you to see now.

"You were muttering the name of Judas when I arrived here. What does Judas mean to you? What does that name mean?"

That was easy. It meant betrayal, Ed told him. Benedict Arnold was a Judas who sold out to what he thought would be the winning side. The Greek shepherd who sold out his fellow Greeks at Marathon to save his hide was a Judas. And by Heaven, Judson K., who sold out for the supposed benefits of a fatter bottom line, was a Judas, too! So what? Wasn't that the point Ed was making in the first place? "Where does that leave us?" Ed was still trying to see Matt's point.

"It leaves you in a new arena. New for you, that is. But, as you pointed out by your little history lesson—Benedict Arnold and all that—it's not new at all. It's the arena of betrayal. It's a hard arena, no doubt about it. But it's the one you have to deal with now before you deal with anything else. Love betrayed demands full attention."

"How about a little revenge thrown in?"

The bitterness of Ed's quip wasn't lost on Matt, but he didn't respond to the question. Instead, he seemed to give a whole new direction to the conversation.

"What do you suppose made Judson do it?" he asked Ed.

Ed pondered for a few minutes, gathered his thoughts to follow this new twist. "His background, I suppose," he answered after a while. "Something in the way he was raised, maybe. We never knew him that well while he was growing up. Something in his psychology."

"Is that what made Judas betray Jesus?"

Again, Ed had to stop and think. Where was Matt leading him with all these questions about Judson and Judas, anyway? It wasn't Ed who was the betrayer, after all. Why didn't Matt go talk to Judson, ask him all these questions?

Matt did not wait for Ed to think any longer. "Is that what made Judas betray Jesus? His psychology? You were right, you know, to compare Judson with Judas. Not that what Judson has done is nearly as enormous as what Judas did. But at its heart, all betrayal is of the same family. But to say it is something in his psychology is to cave in to an old excuse in modern clothing, an obsession we have to tag our behavior with new labels. But in the end, it doesn't hold up, even on its own terms."

Matt got up from his chair and began to pace up and down the way he used to do when he was working out special projects and plans with Ed. But now he was working out something else, something Ed had never really thought deeply about. Now he was talking about the practical meaning of the betrayal of love and friendship.

"Take Judas, for example," Matt continued pacing,

"since you brought him into the picture. If it were just a matter of psychology and background, then there were others in Jesus' close company, his special friends, his apostles, who were better candidates for the role of supreme traitor. Take my own namesake, Matthew. A flinty-hearted tax collector, if there was ever one. You can imagine what he had been like before he met Jesus!"

It flashed through Ed's mind that Matt didn't have to imagine these things anymore; he must know now, for sure. But Matt was already going on.

"Or take Mary Magdalene. How expert she must have been at manipulating men, preying on their weaknesses whenever it suited her, for whatever she wanted.

"Or Nicodemus, the subtle, sophisticated Pharisee. A man of the world. He could have found a hundred reasons and a thousand opportunities to betray Jesus. And what about Thomas, the no-nonsense skeptic, the one man immortalized as 'the doubter'? And Simon Peter and James and John, who wanted Jesus to hurry about proclaiming an earthly kingdom, for the sake of their own dreams of power?"

Matt stopped pacing and stood looking down at Ed. "If psychology and background were the answers, those were the people you would have thought would betray Jesus. Those and so many others.

"But Judas? It must have seemed unlikely to any mortal eye. Let me tell you a little about him, Ed." Matt sounded almost relaxed again, like a man settling in to tell a good story—which, in a way, he was doing.

"Judas came from a prosperous town called Kariot down in the farmland at the very southern tip of Judah. In fact, 'Iskariot' means 'the man from Kariot.' Did you know that, Ed?"

Ed shook his head.

"Neither did I, but since I saw you last, I've learned a good deal! Anyway, in the time of Jesus, Kariot was the last caravan stop before the sandy wastes of the Sinai Desert. Every caravan of every merchant probably had to stop at Kariot for water and provisions. It had a large synagogue, a famous school, a strong fortress, held then by the Romans. It traded richly in its famous wines and its marble.

"Judas came from a prosperous Kariot farm family, a family that had priests and doctors of the Law among its members. He was well educated. He traveled on family business. In fact, that's how he happened to be up north, in Capernaum, when Jesus was there. But my point is, Ed, that if you compare Judas to the people I mentioned before—Matthew, Mary Magdalene, those followers of Jesus—and you just take into account what you call psychology and background, well, you just wouldn't come up with the name of Judas Iskariot as a traitor."

Among the many things Ed would ponder later, after Matt had gone, was that by this time he had become so genuinely intrigued, that he had nearly forgotten about Judson—except for that dull pain of disappointment he still felt at the back of his mind. This question of Judas was becoming a riddle. In those later ponderings of his he would feel rather sure that was what Matt had intended. Riddles and parables can have many things in common, after all.

"Well, then," Ed ventured, "if it wasn't psychology

and all that, maybe Judas just misunderstood Jesus and what he was saying all along. Maybe disappointment had something to do with it. Disappointment can be a very powerful force in a man."

Matt nodded. Yes, that seemed like a pretty good explanation, he agreed. But that still left another important question to explain. "You've read the whole Gospel story," he said, "you know things that very few if any of the men and women around Jesus—even his Apostles—understood in those brief and precious days they spent with him. They squabbled among themselves as to who would be the most powerful and prominent in the kingdom of Jesus. James and John asked him for seats at his right and left when he sat on his throne of glory—power and favor in an earthly kingdom was what they all thought they were achieving with Jesus.

"Simon Peter, the man Jesus himself made the very head of his Apostles, denied Jesus three times out of fear for his own skin. Even after his resurrection, when they had everyone of them touched Jesus, eaten and talked with him, had actually seen the proof and force of his divine power, and when he had won for them a victory and a power beyond all imagining, they still misunderstood. You remember how Mark tells us about it. They walked with the risen Jesus out of Jerusalem to Mount Olivet, where he was to ascend out of their mortal sight into Heaven. And they asked him, after all they had seen and heard—even on that last day he walked as a man among them—they asked him if now was the time he was going to start the new kingdom of Israel! And they meant a political kingdom, with themselves in powerful positions—chief ministers, generals of armies, financial agents, all of that!

"No, Ed. If Judas misunderstood, he wasn't alone in that. They all did. None of those favored men really understood anything about Jesus' mission, about his Church, about his death and resurrection. Not until that almost violently transforming visit by the Holy Spirit at Pentecost, and the showering of special gifts on them. God had to do violence, in a manner of speaking, to their mere human natures. They needed such a transformation, because that was the extent of their weakness and their misunderstanding, and even, as you say, Ed, their disappointment.

"Yet, they never sold Jesus out, however weak and however disappointed they may have been over those three years. And why not? Just one reason, Ed. One reason. They may not have understood Jesus. But they did love him. They loved him too much ever to betray him. They may have been weak. They asked silly questions. They were self-seeking. At times, we know that they were cowardly and frightened. But they loved him. And because they loved him, they trusted what he said, even if they couldn't understand it. Because they loved him, they could not betray him.

"In that love, they could not even imagine such a thing as betrayal. Do you remember that part of the Gospel that tells how Jesus told his Apostles they would betray him? Do you remember how Simon Peter denied that he would ever do such a thing? How they all murmured in their shock that they could not do such a terrible thing? Except for Judas. "Is it I?" Judas asked Jesus. "Yes, it is you," Jesus answered. And Judas made no answer, no protest. He knew that Jesus knew. And he didn't care. Why? Simply because he didn't love Jesus.

"I'll grant you this, though, Ed. I expect Judas misunderstood, all right, and that he was disappointed. And I'll grant you that sets up powerful forces. But the question still is: How do you deal with it all? What are the choices you make, the means you take hold of at the best or worst of times, at any and at all times?

"I mean, Judas saw what Jesus' enemies saw—the adulation of the crowds, the constant seeking out of Jesus by thousands of people. Jesus could command the elements. He could command the people. All he needed to do was issue a call to arms and vast numbers would stream to fight under his banner. It's hard to imagine now, because we don't think of Jesus in that way—and we're right not to. But many did. They thought of him merely as a great man who could have glory and national renown for the taking. It seemed to escape them that he refused and even fled more than one concerted attempt to make him king and to place him at the front of a popular political and military movement.

"But the problem for Judas wasn't that he saw *what* Jesus' enemies saw. Again, so did all the other Apostles, and the disciples. The problem for Judas was that he saw it the *same way* the enemies of Jesus saw it."

Ed's confusion surfaced again. "But these enemies saw Jesus as a threat to their power. Judas wasn't threatened . . ."

Matt sat back in his chair and focused his eyes on the wall, almost as in that portrait, and as though he was watching some scene being played out before his very eyes.

"Yes." Matthew's voice was soft but very clear. "In a way he was threatened. He was the one who bought food and provisions for Jesus and the others. As official hostility to Jesus grew, Judas was probably the first to know it, as tradesmen threw his money back in his face, refused to deal with him. Judas understood things like that, I expect. But the most important similarity between Judas and the enemies of Jesus was that they all seemed to see everything about Jesus without love. Each one of them, I imagine, had his own 'bottom-line' reason: Fear. Power. Conformity. Career. Prestige. Any or all of those, or a dozen others.

"What was missing for Judas was love. Without love, there is no understanding, no trust, not even sheer obedience without understanding. Without love, all of those other things—fear, conformity, greed, prestige—all act on your soul like whirlwinds in the desert. They batter you with biting sands, and blind your eyes, and in the end they leave you confused and parched and exhausted, wondering where you are.

"It's a curious thing, though, Ed. Human history is testimony enough that any man, any woman, can choose to leave those whirlwinds. There is nothing that cannot be forgiven by love. Even Judas' betrayal was no exception. Even having been the direct cause of Jesus' passion and death, Judas could have run to that cross on Calvary, kissed those bleeding feet, wept with his sorrow, joined the pain he surely felt with Jesus' pain, joined Jesus again in love, asked his forgiveness, asked for his blessing as even the stranger, the thief, hanging on the cross beside Jesus, did.

"Even later, he could have joined the Apostles—they had all deserted Jesus. Smaller betrayals, yes, but still betrayals. John, so loved by Jesus in so many ways, ran away from Gethsemane in fear. Simon Peter denied him three

times. Yet Jesus entrusted John with the care of his beloved mother, and Simon Peter with the care of his beloved Church. With them, Judas could have chosen to wait
for that transformation by the Holy Spirit at Pentecost. He
didn't.

"At every point, he chose another path. The path away
from love. And, finally, in his despair and pain, he made
the final choice of alienation from Jesus, of exile from
God. At that point, for him, it no longer mattered what
little motives he might have chosen over love. For Judas,
everything was lost."

Silence consumed time. Perhaps moments passed. Perhaps hours. Ed was almost able to summon before his eyes
the scenes Matt had described to him, almost able to pick
them up like photos, to examine them, search out meanings, look for familiar faces.

When they finally spoke again, it was not about Judas,
the traitor from Kariot, or about the Apostles who might
have been drowned in the backwash of Judas' act. It was
about Jesus. And about love. And about Judson. It was
about Ed himself and the rest of the Lovely Retail family,
the thousands of people who would be affected personally,
one by one, by what Judson K. had done. Jobs would be
lost. There would be financial woes, miseries of all sorts.
People would be paralyzed by the sting of "sectional
analyses," and chewed up by "achievement coordinates"
and spat out by "labor-cost ratios." Most of them wouldn't
even be able to guess at the magnitude of the changes that
were coming. But Ed could. And he could guess, too, that
many in the Lovely Retail family would end up calling the
world a jungle, a loveless refuse heap where scoundrels like

Judson K. get the prize and "poor, stupid, honest folks like us" get the boot.

"What about them?" Ed wanted to know. "They're not Judases. Why should they suffer? And what can they do? What can any of us do?"

"How can anyone survive such betrayal?" Matt repeated the despairing question Ed had asked when he thought he was alone, looking out the window of his office. "You're right. That is the central question now. That is the question that stakes out the arena, the reality in which you will make your choices and decisions, and Judson will make his, and each person in the whole Lovely Retail family will make theirs.

"Let's leave Judson aside for just a minute. Let's look at the choices facing the rest of this company family we have cared so much about, you and I. Many of them, perhaps most of them, will be hurt by what Judson has done, just as you say. They'll be bitter and confused, many of them. Jobs will be lost. Really tough trials will have to be faced by many. They'll curse Judson and anyone else they think is to blame—even you. But I'll tell you one thing—even if this sounds like Pollyanna to you, let me tell you, it's tough—they must keep their souls and spirits clear-eyed enough not to curse love itself, the love and loyalty in which they've lived and worked to this very day. They must not begin to think that it is love that has betrayed them. Because if they do, if they make that decision, and stick to it, they'll be caught up in those same whirlwinds that caught Judson and Judas and too many others.

"Remember this, Ed. Every person in the Lovely Retail family was nurtured and valued in the same spirit Judson was. I don't take credit for that. I always meant what I said: 'Value the things of Heaven.' It was a command, an offer, made to me, and made to everyone else, by God himself.

"Now comes a test. It's not always so easy to make the right choices. It's not always possible to feel love; and the test is whether love is so firm a choice for you, deep down, that even in bitter times, when you can't *feel* love at all, but only pain and anger, you can still trust what love teaches, and you can still obey the lessons love has taught.

"You said it yourself, Ed. Disappointment can set up powerful forces in people's hearts. At some time, each person, even in the depth of his or her disappointment, will find out if, like Matthew or Mary Magdalene or John or Andrew or Simon Peter, they have really learned love, learned it so well, responded to it so completely, that even when it appears to be swept away, they obey its meaning, its lessons. Or if, a bit like Judas, they have not learned love, but only walked with it a while, when it was easy, when things looked bright, and there was not much to frighten them.

"Some may make that latter choice for a while. Run as John ran. Deny love as Simon Peter did. But John came back, stood at the cross, and in a long and painful exile suffered for love of Jesus, wrote the sublimest words about love's meaning and the most fearful words of love's warning that have ever been set down. And Simon Peter came back as well, and died because he finally understood that love is not a bargain for better wages or for power, but a guarantee that any burden, even death, becomes light when carried on love's yoke.

"Those are not easy lessons. But they are easier than the lesson Judas learned. Easier than the lessons of fear, abandonment, despair. Easier than the bitter lessons you plunge into when at every chance you refuse love, or refuse love's pardon.

"And do you know why, Ed? Because that refusal is the sin against the Holy Spirit that Jesus spoke about. Do anything else, then ask forgiveness, and you return to love's friendship. Deny love, however, and you will not even ask. As Judas did not ask. That, finally, is why Jesus did not forgive Judas. Judas never asked.

"No miracle of forgiveness was performed by Jesus unless it was asked for, and asked for with a faith that it would be forthcoming. It's the same today. Christians know that. We know that Jesus is still here. Oh, there are squabbles—very important ones and sometimes very unpleasant ones—about what that means, about how it can be so. But it is so. And, just as he said to many who came to him in Judah and Galilee and Jerusalem, 'Your faith has made you whole,' so now he will say to many who come to him here in this city, in all the cities where the Lovely Retail family members will suffer because of Judson's betrayal, 'Your faith has made you whole.'

"That's the choice, Ed. That has always been the choice. Even in good times, even in all the good years we spent together, the choice was the same. It's just that, in hard times, our own weakness seems to stare us in the eye and frighten us. Love says to us in our weakness: 'Come to me. Ask, and I will strengthen you.'

"Now, of course, some of our family will walk away from that offer of love. Others—you for example—will say, as Simon Peter did, 'To whom shall we go, Lord?' You must help as many of them as you can. Squabble and fight for them with all your strength. And you will pray for them all. Always."

All of what Matt had told him would give Ed much to think about, much to sort out in practical terms. But there was no confusion in his mind; the messages love sends do not have that effect. There was just a great deal to take to heart and to ruminate about in the mind.

And yet, there was still one more question. He had thought of it for just a second, way back when Matt had first started asking those hard questions about Judson and Judas. It was just there at the back of his mind, tickling at the edge of thought. If only he could remember—Yes, that was it!—Judson. Why hadn't Matt gone to Judson to explain all this? It wasn't Ed who was the betrayer. It was Judson. Why hadn't Matt asked all those questions and worked out the answers with Judson himself, then?

"Because," Matt answered him, "like Judas, Judson hasn't asked. It's each person's choice. When you stood over there by that window and said, 'God in Heaven! Who can survive such darkness, such betrayal?,' you were asking an eternal question, and you were asking it out of a fund of faith, of belief, and out of expectation borne of that faith. You were a twentieth-century Simon Peter asking 'To whom shall we go, Lord?' You were the same as the man in the Gospel who pleaded with Jesus, 'Lord, I believe. Help my unbelief.' You were saying you did not have the answer nor the strength to face the hard issue of betrayal. And you were asking for the answer in faith. You expected an answer, because you still have love."

Still, Ed couldn't just write Judson K. off. What Judson had done was terrible. But the parallel with Judas only went so far. Even if every betrayal of love and friendship does reach to Jesus—and Ed agreed that it does—there is still a matter of degree, after all. Betraying the Lovely Retail family was not as huge an offense as betraying Jesus, the Lord of the universe. Ed couldn't just write Judson off.

No, Matt agreed. Ed could not write Judson off. For Judson, it was all still an open question. And the answer lay with Judson himself. "Oh, don't get me wrong," Matt used that familiar cliché for the last time. "Pray for Judson. Talk to him and see if he will listen. Because Judson has heard all the words and learned all the things that you and I did. We helped teach him many things ourselves, if you recall. And," Matt said, rising from his chair in that way he had always done when it was time to end their meetings together, "as long as there is time left to him, you must assume that the choice is there for him to make. That's the one requirement that never changes for anyone. Each one has to make the choice. Help him. Judson only has to ask. Just once. In truth."

❋

Ed rose from his chair and looked at his watch. He didn't remember turning on the lamp. But then he had been so deep in thought! He glanced up at Matthew Lovely's smiling portrait again. Funny that he should feel so close to Matt at just this time when Lovely's Retail was going to change forever.

Well, he'd think about that later. He hadn't realized the time. Past closing. He went to his office door and opened it for the first time since he had stormed through it in his rage at Judson. Everyone was gone, except his assistant, Veronica. She looked at him, as he came through the door.

"You should be gone home by now," he said to her; but he knew why she was still there.

"I was worried, Ed. I'd never seen you like that."

Yes. He knew. That was the way the people of the Lovely Retail family were. "I'm fine now," he smiled his thanks at her. "Are the minutes of the board meeting ready?"

"Not yet, Ed. First thing in the morning."

"Good. That will do. Do you know if Judson is still in his office?"

"I think he is. He came by to see you a few minutes ago, but I told him you weren't to be disturbed. I assumed..."

"Yes, you assumed right, as usual. Do me one favor before you leave, will you, Veronica? Ask Judson if he's free for dinner tonight. Just the two of us. There are a few things he and I haven't discussed in a while. Tell him I'll be waiting in my office for his answer."

The Good
Soldier of Beulah Land

SELFLESS LOVE

WHEN the Reverend Cliffton B. learned from the prestigious Foundation for Religion Sciences that he had been unanimously selected by a panel of his peers as the recipient of the annual John the Baptist Award, it came as the crowning reward of his career as a pastor and an evangelist. And it came as the crowning of his family's much longer history of service and dedication in this land of America.

"For solid achievement," the citation said in part, "in preaching the Word of God and announcing the truths of salvation in season and out of season...."

Reverend Cliff, as he was fondly called by his parishioners, felt he was at an age and a stage of mind where he could most deeply appreciate this award. Twenty-five years before this, he would have taken it as something different, something that would open doors of flattering success, a spur to more intense activities that would bring ever greater recognition. But, mature now in faith and in age, he was no longer fascinated by the tinsel of publicity or caught up in a feverish activism. He had been through all that.

He knew, of course, that the award would bring him wide recognition and acclaim. There would be guest lectures and interviews; his sermons would be sought after for publication; there would be substantial and very welcome donations for his church, the Church of the Savior set in the rolling prairie lands of his beloved America. But in his eyes now, all of that paled in importance beside the two greatest reasons for his joy and satisfaction at receiving the award.

The first was his own deep admiration of the supreme model of John the Baptist. His acceptance speech for this award would give him a huge public forum in which he could summarize for his fellow Americans and his fellow Christians all he had discovered about the Good News and about the great evangelist who had prepared its way.

The second was that, as it seemed to Cliff, life's most rewarding dream had come true for him. Not only had the Church founded by Jesus bent down and showered him with special blessing: "Well done, good and faithful servant!" Not only had the people of God turned to him and praised him: "The Lord has been in your heart, and his words of life have been on your lips." It was his return for a life invested in love. It was love's return. It was a visible proof and a public celebration of what he so often preached to his own flock: "If you love God and your fellow man, it's like an investment. It has a return—and with interest."

Yet, it was not his return alone, as he well knew. Reverend Cliff came from a family that had given many men

to the church, and he saw the award not only as the cul-
mination of his personal career, but a recognition for all
his family's service. Even with the deluge of congratula-
tory mail and phone calls, the burst of publicity and the
waves of prestige that began to break agreeably upon him,
still, in the few weeks he had to prepare his acceptance
speech, his mind often traveled back over the history of his
family, which had paralleled so closely the history of
America.

He recalled the stories of his ancestors who had come to
this land in a 55-foot sloop called the *Susan Constant*.
They landed at Chesapeake Bay on April 26, 1607. They
had a clear and shining hope, and they never doubted or
betrayed that hope: To find Beulah Land. And the meaning of that hope for them was what it had been for the
ancient Israelites who were the first to sing about a dream
they had and a hope they nourished: To reach Beulah
Land. *Beulah* in Hebrew means "husbanded" or "cherished." For Cliff's forebears as for the Israelites, their
dreamland would be a land cherished by God. The promise made by God himself was that their wandering across
seas and continents would bring them to a land that he had
cherished and loved as a husband does his own wife; a land
that they would love as God had loved it; a land in which
they would serve him, and he would be their God. For he
had loved them enough to lead them there.

"Mansions are prepared for me," the new pilgrims
sang. "The Angels take me by the hand and show me
Heaven's tableland. Beulah Land! Beulah Land!"

Those were the words, and that was the hope, with
which Cliffton B.'s ancestors had worked and prayed and

devoted their lives to God for nearly four hundred years. Over the decades and the centuries, they moved inland. North and south and west, they endured the hardships of the colonizers, the pioneers, the farmers, the hardworking men and women who also came to claim God's gift and great reward.

Each new place they went, his family built their houses of worship before they built their living quarters. For it was upon the foundation stones of their churches that they hoped to secure as well the foundations of faith, help to spread a glory of Light over this new people, this new America, this place husbanded for them by God. Beulah Land!

And so it was not only with his own joy and gratitude that Cliff devoted himself so completely to the preparation of his acceptance speech. It truly seemed to him that, eloquent though he was in his unemotional way, he must borrow upon the eloquence of all those who had come before him in his line, that he must give tribute for them as well as himself to the great prophet of the desert, in whose footsteps of faith they had walked. He must accept for them all, as well as for himself, this vindication of their hope and their vision, this reward for their love.

The last few days before the award ceremonies, Cliff's wife, Julia, tried her best to see that he was not disturbed. She knew how great a tribute Cliff wanted his speech to be. Even his three children, grown and with their own families now, were advised gently by the wise Julia to make few demands on his time until the award ceremonies were over and done with.

It was all worth it, for all of them. Cliff's performance

was magnificent. His central theme was the Baptist's own: "I baptize you in water. But there is one coming after me who will baptize you in fire and the Spirit of Holiness. . . ." He declaimed upon that fire and that spirit as the signs of true Christianity, the harbingers of love and the hope of love, that open the doors of Heaven for us. He declaimed upon the Baptist, the greatest evangelist of all time, "the greatest man born of woman," as Jesus himself had stated. "I am the voice of one crying in the wilderness," he quoted the Baptist's own description of himself, and added, "crying out about love in the wilderness."

For thirty-five minutes, Cliff held his audience spellbound and brought them finally to their feet, some of them in tears, all in delirious acclaim. The smiling faces of his wife and his children in the front row were radiant and eloquent proof of his success. Truly, this was his supreme moment of earthly reward.

When it was all over, and at last the brouhaha had died down, Cliff was ready to settle back into his normal life as pastor at the Church of the Savior in the middle of the rolling prairies. In fact, it seemed to him most fitting that this place his ancestors had helped to clear and to build with their sweat and in their faith, should be his home for the rest of his days. Nor was there any letdown of his spirit or his emotions. For the fact that he, the pastor of a rather rural community, had been picked for the award endeared his community all the more to him. Its members loved him and he loved them. Again and again in his sermons, he chose examples from among this very flock to show how, each day, love of God and of your fellow man is like an investment that brings a return of goodness.

Love with a return, he often said to them, is not a selfish ideal. In fact, he reasoned for them, with some little experience and basic good will, we all know that the return on love cannot be fifty-fifty all the time or in all circumstances. It varies, because a living love in the heart of a living human has its peaks and valleys, all of them acceptable, enjoyable even, as making up the substance of love. But if, with our love, we also have patience, he said, the variations do not matter; for over time they must even out. So we believe and so we live our lives. If ours is a truly living love, if we can count on that return on our love, then we can face anything in this life.

But, he admonished in wise and gentle warning, if we do not have that living return on our investment of love, life does not seem worth living. As in the love of a man and a woman joined in marriage, without the presence of the beloved, there is no return possible. The beautiful light that only love gives, is extinguished. Nothing, not memories or photographs, not mementos—a lock of hair, a poem, an old letter—not a change of scenery, nothing can set that light shining again. But, he said, when we speak of our Lord Jesus, we are never without his presence. As long as we love him, there will be a return for our investment of love.

Cliff's congregation could see for itself how right he was. The people of his community followed that spiritual vision of his as best they could, and everything about them —their city, their streets, their homes—all did seem to be illumined with daily returns on their love. Oh, there were a few tarnished edges here and there. Edges of dissatisfaction, impatience. But, after all, these were the closing years of a turbulent century in an impatient land. And, after all, didn't the exceptions only prove the rule? Love has its return. Abandon love and you forfeit love's return.

Had it been left to Cliff, he would surely have finished out his active life, lived for God and for God's people, in that little community that surrounded the Church of the Savior where he enjoyed and gave a love clearly blessed by Jesus. But, as Cliff himself would observe in a time not that far distant, love has other dimensions, further reaches, in which anyone might suddenly be called upon to attain a higher degree of holiness. There lay ahead of this man of God a time in which he would learn a little of the harder wisdom of love: "Whom the Lord loves, he chastises."

It seemed coincidental, a flattering but otherwise unremarkable invitation made to Cliff by a special committee of his peers during the annual meeting of pastors. The award he had received, his fellow clergymen told him, only pointed in bold relief to what they already knew. He would be the perfect man to take over a congregation they felt to be in considerable difficulty. It wasn't money that was the problem. In fact, it was quite a sizable and well-heeled congregation that didn't lack for funds. But their church had fallen on bad times spiritually. The previous pastor had just died. A good man, they told Cliff, and a dedicated professional churchman. But he had neglected the preaching of the Word and religious instruction, in his zeal to put the church on that sound financial footing it now enjoyed. "You see," they explained, "the congregation is one of the new planned communities, not more than a dozen years old, built from scratch, you might say. There was the financing and building of the church to attend to, and all of those things. But the problem we face in our search for his successor is to find a man who will

enliven the church he built with that very Word, that instruction, that has been lacking there. To invest the bricks
and mortar, so to speak, with Spirit."

"But why ask me?" Cliff wanted to know, "a man in
the twilight of his life and his career?"

"Well," one of his peers took on the role of spokesman,
"for one thing, your family has always moved with the new
pioneers of this God-given land, and as we said, this is a
new community. These people aren't pioneers in the sense
your ancestors were. But in another sense, they are on the
edge of a new frontier in their own way. They need you as
much as the Church of the Savior has needed you. And,"
he smiled, "it seemed to us that Jesus himself has pointed
to you. You see, the church in the new community is called
the Church of St. John the Baptist."

Once back at home, Cliff thought and prayed deeply
about what he should do; and he talked it over with Julia.
The more he thought and prayed and discussed, the more
he thought about the coincidence that the new church was
called after the Baptist. He was wise enough to probe
deeply what seemed outwardly to be merely one of the
accidental happenings of life. Very often these form the
very crossroads of opportunity that fashion our way on the
narrow path to God. He knew that Jesus rarely sends an
angel to advise his loved ones. Nor does he normally speak
to them in dreams of the night. He speaks, like the omni-
potent God that he is, through events, favorable and
unfavorable, pleasant and unpleasant, welcome and unwelcome. Cliff began to read this offer as a silent message
from the Baptist himself whose award had made such a
difference in his life. It was as if he could imagine the
fiery Baptist himself saying to him: "Do you think you re-

ceived that award only for your own delight, your own enjoyment?" No, Cliff was meant to serve for all his days, as John had served for all of his.

If Julia B. had been less of a wife, less loving a supporter of her husband's calling, she would have had ample reason to object even to considering such a move. She had been born in this prairie community, had all her roots and most of her friends and her family nearby. But from the very beginning, when Cliff had first told her of the offer, she knew that, even though they might find a thousand reasons to stay at the Church of the Savior, and a thousand more for not undertaking a new mission, Cliff was, before anything else, a devoted servant of Jesus. He was what Paul had called his friend Timothy: "The good soldier of Christ Jesus." In her mind, "the good soldier" was already on his way to the new assignment.

The Church of St. John the Baptist was just as it had been described. It was set in the heart of a new community planned and built for people with a certain amount of money. The community had its own security force, a handsomely landscaped layout, public monuments, parks, public transport, its own shopping complexes and supermarkets, its own movie houses and even a lively community hall and auditorium. It was kept immaculately clean. There were no slums, and little crime to speak of.

The church itself, which served a parish of about three thousand registered members, was a mirror of its setting. On the surface everything seemed fine. On the day of their arrival, the parish council welcomed Cliff and Julia warmly: They had good money in the bank and they had offered him generous recompense. Only right, they insisted, for a man of the Reverend Cliffton B.'s status and reputation. They showed him the church property. The church building itself was a bit stark and modern, Cliff thought, but ample in its provisions. It did seem, though, that the auditorium and community hall were much larger than the church itself. "For fund-raising activities, Reverend," one of the council explained. "And for dances and such events for the young people," one of the mothers in the group took up. "A place where we felt they'd stay out of trouble and have a good time without feeling we were watching over them, you know."

At the council dinner where Cliff was officially received as pastor of the Church of John the Baptist, the head of that all-powerful council rose and spoke the mind of all its members. "We welcome you as the bowknot, the golden hasp, that holds this loving community together."

"With all my heart," Cliff had stood in his turn and responded with warmth, "I shall be your pastor, and guide you in the Word and the Spirit of the Lord Jesus."

And with all his heart, Cliff felt, he really did try to do exactly that. True, the first few Sundays, his congregation was quite small. But, as Julia pointed out, it was still late summer, and many parishioners were surely away on vacation.

By the time summer was clearly over, however, Cliff began to suspect why the community hall was so much larger than the church. At "coffee-and-buns" get-togethers and "Las Vegas Nights," and other imaginative fundraisers, he met and at least superficially got to know more of his congregation than he ever saw from the pulpit of John the Baptist Church.

Of course, he and Julia were welcomed into the homes of many, many people in the community. In fact, cocktail

parties and dinners seemed to be the centerpiece around
which everything important revolved. Inevitably, there
was an unspoken but well-understood ranking, a pecking
order, as Julia phrased it, in such a community. Families
were graded in importance according to the suspected size
of their bank accounts, the panache of their homes, the
importance of honored guests they could secure for special
evenings. Cliff and Julia were entertained by each family,
it seemed, but in its pecking order, until they felt they
would love nothing better than a month without a social
invitation.

At Sunday services, however, the same four or five
hundred people turned up, some one Sunday, others the
next. About a sixth of the total parish, by Cliff's reckoning,
attended church. Very few of their constant dinner hosts
were among them. He got to know some of these regulars
quite well. They were nice people, good people, fun loving, generous with their hospitality and their regular contributions. They were proud of their church and of their
new, distinguished pastor. A few of them were even remarkably devout, visiting the church for occasional lone
vigils, visiting Cliff to ask for guidance and prayer in this
situation or that.

There was one woman he took especially to his heart
when he found her at prayer one day by herself, kneeling
in one of the pews. She was so frail that her body seemed
like a child's. When he approached her, she tried to stand
in a respectful greeting, but he saw the effort it cost her;
and, instead, he sat down beside her for a while. She had a
little bandage above one eye, and her clothes, though clean
and well made, were not pressed. Cliff asked her name.
Edna, she told him. She had been ill, she said. Her family

had found her a little house in this lovely town where they were sure she would be safe and happy and tranquil. But they were so busy, life now was so hectic, she smiled, they rarely had a chance to visit with her. The bandage? Oh, nothing, just a little fall when she had tripped on a curb. One of the security people, a very nice young man, had helped her to a clinic. God was good, she beamed. Her house was close enough for her to walk to John the Baptist from time to time. And she was so happy that Reverend Cliff didn't lock the doors during the week, as his predecessor had always done. "It's a comfort for me to come here when I feel strong enough," she confided.

Cliff and Julia took to visiting Edna. Each day one of them would be sure to stop by with some portion of choice food and with love to share; and Julia saw to it, in her unobtrusive way, that the cleaning and the ironing and the cooking were done for her. Edna was always so happy to see them; but she didn't want to be a bother. She was no bother; she was, Cliff thought, the loveliest person he had met in years, a trusting child among children of Christ. And her simple faith was the closest thing he'd found to love's return in his first several months at John the Baptist.

After Cliff had got to know as many members of his church as he felt he ever would in the present circumstances, and after he had got to know the rhythms of their lives, the pressures on them, and their responsiveness to the currents of thoughts and feelings that eddied around them, he felt it was time to begin to keep his promise, to begin to be "their pastor," as he had said at the council dinner, "and to guide them in the Word and the Spirit of the Lord Jesus."

The most immediate means he had, of course, were his

Sunday sermons. He was an evangelist, after all, and the award of John the Baptist was not only a tribute to that fact, but was at least partly what had made this community keen to have him here. He would make his sermons urbane and entertaining to fit their taste, and yet he would fill them with the light of Jesus' love. He hoped that the fraction of his congregation who came to listen to him on Sundays would carry the word, tell others who would come in their turn and hear him, and then attract still others.

Cliff threw himself with great fervor into the preparation of those sermons. He preached as he had never preached on the prairies. He gave examples of the love of God. He spoke with controlled feeling of the holiness in God's love; of the pursuit of goodness within that love as the core and the greatness of America; and of the return we all receive in God's love and in the blessings of Jesus. He spoke, in other words, of the "hundred-fold reward" that Jesus promised would accrue to his faithful servants for their fidelity to his commandments.

And, indeed, people did remark on those sermons, as Cliff had hoped. It was plain to see, they nodded approvingly, why he had been singled out for the award of John the Baptist. Weren't they lucky to have him! Wasn't it fortunate that they could afford the best! But, if attendance increased by much, Cliff didn't see it. Another hundred souls would have been a generous guess.

Church attendance was not the only problem to trouble Cliff. He was deeply disturbed by the local habit—fast becoming tradition here—of holding the holiest and the most important celebrations of life away from the holy place of God—this church of John the Baptist. Marriages, for example, were held by the central fountain in the park, in ceremonies that were about as religious as a picnic. A marriage was as much a marriage, the people said, whether they said the words by a fountain or in a stuffy church. And what was the difference if a young couple wrote their own marriage vows? On that point, Cliff might have asked what marriage meant, because couples so often seemed to exchange vows that amounted to "we will be faithful for as long as we are faithful." He might have asked, but he didn't.

It was the same in everything. Not even memorial services or prayer services before burial were held in church with any regularity. Cliff was made to understand by the council—politely, of course, for these were good people who had no wish to offend—that he would be welcome to officiate "on all of these occasions, wherever they might be observed." Was he not, after all, the bowknot of their happy community?

Over the months, a tug of wills began between Cliff and members of his official congregation—both the regular and the infrequent churchgoers—until inevitably real friction began to develop with the council itself. He began to worry and wonder, as Julia did, if he would be confirmed in his post at the end of his first year at John the Baptist. He did not want to leave here, to fail for the first time in his long evangelist ministry. But in another sense he did not want to be confirmed in the post for the wrong reasons.

Well, there were still many months before his first year would be over. He still had time to think, to pray, to work for love's reward even in this—what had that committee spokesman called this place? Oh, yes, this "new frontier in its own way."

It was in just that spirit of working for love's reward

that Cliff told Julia he had decided to do something special for his new people. "Christmas is coming," he said to Julia. "Surely that is a time for God's people to draw together with him and with each other." With his own money, because he wanted to surprise the council and his new community, he purchased a life-size replica of the first Christmas—the holy family and the shepherds and the animals, and the three Wise Men, all beautifully crafted and sculpted. He would have it placed at the front of the church. And he would prepare a very special Christmas Eve homily for them. He would at least begin the Christmas celebration where it belonged—in the holy place of God. Then, carols would be sung outside around the huge lighted Christmas tree that had been the only visible celebration ever made in this parish for the season of Jesus' birth. With this change, with the crèche and the Word of God preached as these people had rarely heard it, and with the help of Jesus, maybe he would make them see just a little of what Christmas meant. That was his deepest wish, his constant prayer. For he was by now deeply concerned for the spiritual welfare of this little community of three thousand souls perched on the edge of a new frontier.

The council *was* very surprised. But the council did not approve. "It is very pretty, as you say," the president said. He had to concede that much in all fairness; but no more. The idea of a crèche was childish, the council was in firm agreement. That was why they never had had one.

Cliff was caught totally off guard. It had seemed so perfect an idea, so perfect a time to make an offering of peace and try to begin anew. He had not anticipated any objection. He sat in that meeting of the council, the crèche figures displayed around the room, and he was speechless.

And then, for the first time, he began to understand. In fact, understanding seemed to sweep over him like an icy tide. "Do you . . ." His voice cracked. He had to clear his throat and start again. "Tell me, do you celebrate Christmas as the birth of God? The birth of God as a helpless child? The birth of God from a real, human mother?"

The council members exchanged glances, but no one spoke for a minute. Cliff would remember that as one of the longest minutes he had spent in years. When finally one of the council answered, it was no answer at all. Just words about having a very integrated community here and maintaining standards consistent with "how we have evolved in a godly way of life." There were placating words: Some people would surely feel as Cliff did about having a crèche. And there were warning words: Others would not feel that way at all. As they had explained to Cliff from the beginning, he was expected to be the knot that bound the community together, taking no sides, but "catering to all aspects of that godliness."

"If Jesus wishes us to see it differently," the council president added, "ask him to help us see that. God knows, we need help."

With that makeshift request for their pastor's prayers, the council meeting was hastily adjourned, and its members left just as hastily without the usual pleasantries and chatter.

Cliff sat alone there for some time feeling every moment more like a master of civil ceremonies, or a highly paid secretary-general to a larger-than-normal country club. "I am a pastor!" His voice was hoarse with emotion in the empty room. "I preach Jesus, true God and true man! If I don't do that, then I am nothing!"

In the end, Cliff set up his Christmas crèche in the church, and the town set up the huge tree on the lawn outside and decorated it with merry lights and a great star. There was no Christmas Eve homily. Cliff and Julia joined the many who came on Christmas Eve to sing carols around the tall tree and the many more who came for refreshments in the hall.

The congregation on Christmas Day was much reduced. Edna, that trusting child of God, was there among the worshipers. She must have been the frailest of all Cliff's parishioners, he thought that Christmas Day, and the most alone in any usual sense. But she was the one about whom he had to worry least. He smiled at her where she sat very near his crèche.

As Cliff looked around his church, its pews half empty on Christmas, he knew that the quiet struggle had been heightened between him and this congregation. Hardly a war, but certainly a struggle.

War, in fact, did not erupt till spring. When it did erupt, it was about a baptism. As usual, Cliff had tried to persuade the parents to hold the baptism in the church. As usual, they refused. As usual, he performed the ceremony in the open air by the fountain.

The godparents were almost as fresh and attractive as the infant girl who was to be baptized. They were a young couple Cliff had married the previous year in that very spot. He hadn't seen them since, and he chatted with them a bit. They were fine, they said, smiling their fresh, attractive smiles.

The young godmother took the infant from its mother and Cliff began the ceremony.

"Are you willing," Cliff asked, moving into the ancient

ritual, "to watch over this little girl as your godchild, to care for her health of mind and body, to see that she knows and loves her Christian faith, to guide her so that she stays within the friendship of the Lord Jesus?"

"We are," her godparents answered solemnly.

Cliff then started the essential declarations of belief in the truths of Christianity, to be answered by the god-parents on behalf of the infant.

"Do you believe in God, the creator of the Universe?"

"We do."

"Do you believe in Jesus Christ as Savior and as Lord?"

When there was no reply, Cliff looked up from the book of ritual from which he was reading out the ques-tions. There was an awkward silence, then a bit of hurried whispering between parents and godparents.

It was the young godmother who answered the ques-tion, but not in the usual way. "That's an awful lot to lay on us just like that, Reverend Cliffton," she said in a pip-ing, nervous sort of voice.

"Yes," her young husband came to her aid. "Can't we skip the church frills and just get on with it?"

Cliff went white. He didn't answer either of them. The silence was deathly. In that moment, there were no more questions to ask. He knew. They were not Christians. There could be no baptism that wouldn't be a lie flung in the face of the Holy Spirit. Cliff would not, could not do that. As pastor, as evangelist, as Christian, he could not do that. No one could do that.

It was Julia who noticed two regular churchgoers among the guests. As tactfully as the explosive situation would allow, she smoothed the hasty change, inviting them to be the substitute godparents. Cliff completed the baptism and he left before the outdoor reception began.

The father of the baby girl caught up with him at the edge of the crowd of guests. "I hope you understand, Reverend. . . ."

Cliff turned cold yet burning eyes on the young man. "I thought I had," he interrupted. "I'm sorry. I was wrong. I thought you were Christians."

That day, for the first time in the nine months or so since they had come to the Church of John the Baptist, Julia said aloud what she had barely allowed herself to think. "We had better start looking for a new assignment."

"Perhaps," Cliff said.

As they moved toward Easter, the number attending regular services dropped by a good half. Visitors to Cliff's study asking advice and counsel diminished to a trickle. He had ample time and ample reason to think, to pray. And a new fear he had never experienced before, had never even thought possible for him, began to grow: The fear of defeat. He was beaten. He had failed. He could not understand why or how it had happened. He knew this is an imperfect world. That was why Jesus had come into it. And he knew society often takes its revenge, punishes its chief wrongdoers, locks them up, even; excludes them from its normal life. But why Cliff? Why exclude him? For that is what failure meant. He was excluded from the community he had come to serve and to lead in Jesus' Word and will. He was excluded from his ministry, from his very life.

In the few days remaining before Easter, Cliff made no preparations for its communal observance at the Church of

John the Baptist. Rather, he remained in his study, in fear of his failure, searching for its reasons. He read sermons he had given, speeches he had made. He listened to the tape recording of the award speech. He read manuals, studied the Bible. He was burying himself in the past, searching in its dust for the glory and the rewards Jesus rains upon his people.

Julia knew better than to disturb Cliff in his study that day, even for meals, or to let others distract him. What she could not know was the path of prayer and enlightenment along which Jesus was about to lead her beloved Cliff.

Failure and reward. Those were the two prongs of the painful vise in which Cliff had been caught.

In brooding and praying about his quandary, Cliff was doing no more than emphasizing a concept shared by most of us about failure and reward in love: Whether it is God's love for us, or ours for him, or our human loves, part of love and of loving is that it does bring a return of goodness. It's a concept that not only makes sense, but seems verifiable in our normal Christian lives. Yet, at times, the formula doesn't seem to hold. Some terrible crisis, some awful trial, some unbearable loss, some abject failure or deprivation is thrust upon us; and though we have not deserved it, we cannot seem to escape once it has set its hold on us. Love's return does not apply to us, we say at those moments, in bitter complaint to God.

For Cliff, the failure he thought he saw, the failure he contemplated alone in his study, was specific. Yet, it involved his whole life and its entire meaning. "I preach Jesus, true God and true man!" he had said on that disappointing Christmas when he had been deserted by the council. "If I cannot do that, then I am nothing." And it was in precisely that, that he had now failed.

It is easy to see, however, that Cliff's torment is not so different from our own. Not every Christian is or can be a minister or a preacher; but every Christian is a man or woman of God. If we cannot be that, then we are nothing. And so, the moments in which we perceive ourselves as abandoned by God, by his love, are moments in which we search fearfully for our own part in the failure of love, and in which we accuse God at the same time of punishing us, of taking some revenge of love on us, of excluding us from some important part of our own lives which hitherto he has ratified and blessed.

For Cliff there was a further question. He was a minister of God's word; and he had come to preach that word to a people who had wanted him in their midst, and who had welcomed him. What he had not perceived was exactly what his peers had told him in so many words: These people *were* on the edge of a new frontier, in their own way. It was not the frontier shores of Beulah Land that his ancestors had crossed. But it was, perhaps, the farthest edge of Beulah Land that these people now approached, a place from which they could see into a new land, not of passionate daily belief, and of action based on that belief, but of complacency, of conformity, of cooperation and connivance with any corruption, as long as it observed the outward formulas of "goodness," and no matter that there would be no meaning deeper than getting along without making needless problems. The new frontier on which these people of the Church of John the Baptist now stood gave them an unobstructed view of a land where Cliff and all the ministers and priests of God would fear to tread. A place where the dream of Beulah Land—bride of God, husbanded and cherished by Jesus, an expanse where he would lead them and be their Lord—all of that would, seemingly, be left behind; or at best would seemingly be carried as a dimming memory into a somber and ever-darkening tomorrow.

I say *seemingly* left behind, *seemingly* to be carried only as a dimming memory. And I say that, because herein lies the real dilemma for Christians—and not only for Christian preachers—of today.

No American Christian who has thought his religious belief through, and who has thought his American identity through, would want to see the Congress of these United States amend the Constitution to declare this nation by secular law to be a Christian nation and by secular law to be consecrated to Jesus Christ. Nor would he want to see the president and Congress, supported by the Supreme Court of the United States, pass secular laws enforcing strictly Christian beliefs and practices on each and every American citizen. For the American mind of today, that is unthinkable. In the American mind, no form of religion should be imposed or specially fomented by the United States.

But all Americans should be free to practice the religion of their choice without prejudice, without hindrance, without interference from government. A corollary of that freedom is the freedom to practice no religion—if someone so wishes.

For let us make no mistake about it. Whether we be Protestant, Catholic, Jew, Muslim, Hindu, Buddhist, or unbeliever; whether we be black, white, yellow, or red, male or female; whether we spring from those who came here earliest, or who fought the Revolution and wrote the Constitution, or those who fought the Civil War and two world wars—we all have wanted to ensure one thing: the permanence and the prosperity of this land as the final stepping-stone, for themselves and for millions more who would come after them, to a peculiar freedom. A freedom in religious and moral matters. A freedom according to which there would never be a *Thou Shalt*, never a *Thou Shalt Not*, but only a *Thou Mayest*. Freedom to choose to do good—or evil. But freedom. The choice to do good must be free. The choice for Jesus and his love must be free.

We are still struggling to achieve that freedom in its visible and tangible perfection. We Americans are still struggling and quarreling over this basic meaning of America.

In the meanwhile, Cliff felt, as many other Christian Americans do today, that the values and principles of Christian life were being banished from American life. There can be no doubt that, according to many today, it is un-American to call America a Christian nation. There can be no doubt, furthermore, that many wish, and work to ensure, that Christianity will find no expression in our public marketplace, in our laws, in our educational system, in our treatment of the unborn as well as of the dying, the sick, the aged, the insane. And, it is a peculiar thing about this American freedom of ours that it would seem to be their democratic right to think in this fashion and to endeavor to achieve such goals.

What such industrious anti-Christians do not choose to see, and what nags and gnaws at Christians like Cliffton B., is the subtle but undeniable fact that, if you remove the

Christian moral value from, say, education or from the rules of behavior, you have to replace it with another moral value. You cannot leave a vacuum. There is no escape from that.

To take a farfetched example: If, tomorrow, you pass a law wiping out monogamy in marriage, then you have immediately replaced monogamy with bigamy and polygamy as the law of the United States. You have at the same time replaced the religious underpinning of the law of monogamy with one of two moral assumptions. Either you assume that bigamy and polygamy are acceptable to God; or, you assume there is no God and that, therefore, we humans are quite free to marry simultaneously as many partners as we like. In any case, you impose beliefs even on those who believe the very opposite, and you justify that act awkwardly and dishonestly with the argument that one must not impose beliefs on those who believe the opposite.

Similarly, if through the Department of Education you impose a teaching of evolution in which it is believed and taught that, body and soul, human beings come solely from lower animals that, in turn, come solely from inanimate chemicals which, in their turn, happened along by pure chance, you are imposing the belief that God did not create the soul, that in fact there is no God, that there is no soul.

The same holds true for all of the most torturing questions that divide Americans today—abortion, contraception, homosexuality, pornography, atomic weapons, nuclear energy—to cite only some of the major current issues. Our attitude on each of these questions presupposes a moral viewpoint that may or may not be Christian, and that reflects that moral viewpoint onto the fabric of day-to-day life.

Now, without doubt, there was a time—and very recently, as time goes—when the laws and practices of this land reflected basic Christian principles. The anguish of the Reverend Cliffton B. and of Christians like him, is that slowly but surely this land is being persuaded to replace the Christian ideal, however imperfectly it may have been expressed and lived, with pointedly un-Christian principles and beliefs. Christians see this secularization, as they call it, creeping in everywhere. And, true enough, the day-to-day life of America is changing radically.

At the very same time that the Christian ideal is being excavated from beneath our social values and our laws, something must be put in its place. Something must hold this land together, keep it from disintegrating into a chaos of me-first "isms." And so, all of us have seen and been disturbed by the very visible beginning of a regimentation of life in America—family life, personal life, social life, political life—that at times seems to be the earliest fulfillment of the horror outlined almost forty years ago by the farseeing George Orwell in his famous book *1984*, a portrait of a world in which God no longer exists and all human beings are slaves of the superstate.

Where Christians and religious authorities like the Reverend Cliffton B. go astray is in seeking redress of this situation by merely political means or social formulas. The experience of the ages—since long before America was America—has been that any religion that depends upon a political system, not only rises and falls with the fortunes of that system, but is inevitably and finally secularized and prostituted for purely secular and temporal goals.

The answer lies in a rededication by Christians to the fountain and source of their strength: the love of God as manifested in his son, Jesus Christ. For Jesus is Love itself appearing in history as the master of history, as the Messiah of all our human hopes, and as the savior of all humankind.

A Christian must still preach a message of *Thou Shalt* and *Thou Shalt Not*, even to those who disagree with him, but always as an option behind which will stand the American, *Thou Mayest*.

In this climate particularly, we must know and display the reason for our faith. And we must so live our lives under the banner of Christ's love, that our message becomes winsome and attractive, and the grace of the all-powerful Jesus so empowers our moral and spiritual authority that one day, in the peace and free exchange of America, men and women will turn to us and say the words of Moses' vision: "What great nation has statutes and decrees that are as just as this?"

❋

It was the bleak frontier of that Orwellian world that Cliff and his little congregation had encountered.

As Cliff sat alone in his study searching for solace and for answers in the dust of the past, he remembered the uneasy request for his prayers that the president of the council had made to him: "If Jesus wishes us to see it differently," he had said to Cliff, "ask him to help us see that. God knows, we need help." In other words, he had asked his pastor to function as a pastor, not as a social leader, and not as a political thinker.

And so it was that Cliff's quest for answers began to

change. He knelt alone in the quiet refuge of his study, and he prayed.

"My Lord Jesus, I do not ask you for anything. Good things you have given me. You know the limits of my strength to bear difficulties. I know you want these people for your own. I haven't been able to lead them to you. I haven't been able even to make them see they're headed away from you. I do not deserve any special consideration myself. But these are your people, the people of John the Baptist's church. Because of your saint, John the Precursor, the one who announced you, because of him, Lord Jesus, help me! Help your people! Help your church. In your holy name and for your holy name's sake. Amen."

Nothing pleases God more than a humble heart. Cliff's prayer came from his deep feelings of inadequacy, from his realization that of himself he was nothing and could do nothing. He had had a first glimpse of how self-centered his efforts had been. Once he opened his mind and spirit in this childlike way, it seemed no task at all for the grace of Jesus to bring him swiftly, silently to a real communication with Jesus, with his Father, and with the saints and holy ones who are with Jesus and his Father in eternity.

It began simply, in the most natural manner. Cliff began again to examine in his mind the almost-failed baptism of that baby girl. The choice that had faced him then was a perfect model of the overall dilemma he faced. On that day, he had been expected to make Christian baptism into a charade, a sham, and so betray himself and the child and God. But every day, in a dozen ways, had not his choice been to make Christianity itself into a sham? Or to go against the will of the congregation? It was impossible to see a solution. Either they would desert him—as they were doing—or he would leave them. Or both. Anyway you looked at it, he would fail in his mission here.

It was ironic, he mused, that at this very church of the Baptist, it had been a baptism that had been his final undoing. It was not a bitter thought. Rather, it led him to review all he knew about the Baptist, to examine John's life and the effect of his preaching, his heralding of God's arrival in the midst of humankind.

Then, imperceptibly, this examination became prayer. Prayer became absorption. Absorption became complete until somehow within his very soul he was in the presence of that man whom Jesus called the greatest man ever born of woman. John the Baptist, like all those who belong to Jesus and who have passed into God's eternity, shares every moment of Jesus' solicitude for those who are still here on Earth seeking—sometimes desperately, sometimes joyously, always hopefully—to do the will of Jesus' Father.

Cliff had no vision. He heard no words. But, if ever he were to try to describe what happened to him in his study that day, it would have to be in terms of images and exchanges of thoughts that amount to a conversation. Everything around him remained normal. He could remember the sound of the chiming clock, but he paid it no heed in that special time. He was aware of everything usual around him—but also of something more, or of someone else, as well.

He knew who it was. It was as if he could see him. As if he could hear him and be heard by him. As if he himself actually said, "I have been waiting for you, hoping you would come."

And it was as if John the Baptist, though now living

with Love Itself, had nevertheless taken up the conversation in the most natural way: "Prayers are answered. One way or another, they are always answered!"

"Yes," Cliff agreed. He knew that much. That was what he had always preached. Prayers are answered. Love has its reward. Seek and you shall find.

John shook his head. Cliff couldn't have explained how he knew that, but he did. "Prayers are answered," the Baptist repeated, "but you don't seem to have been listening. Not lately. That's why I'm here. To bring you back to reality."

Cliff had to smile at that. He was quite aware that there were many who would scoff at this entire conversation as unreal. But Cliff had no doubts, and he would not let himself be distracted by worldly asides. He had wanted the Baptist to come—in a way, had asked for him to come—to teach him whatever it was that he so badly lacked now. He would not be cheated of that chance. He began as everyone must, with what he knew.

"My reality," he said to John, "has been the reality you yourself preached. The reality of glorious love. The reality of loving commitment to Jesus and to one another in his love. . . ."

"And," John interrupted, "of a return on love. Of love as an investment."

"Was that wrong?" Cliff was confused. "Didn't the Lord himself tell us to ask in order to receive, to seek and we would find, to knock and it would be opened to us?"

"No." John smiled again, and Cliff wondered that a man who had been so fiery in his life and work would be so gentle. "That was not wrong. It is not wrong for most people, most of the time. But now, *you* are being asked by

Jesus to give him a degree of love you have not yet even imagined."

"Here?" Cliff was incredulous. "Here at the Church of John the Baptist? These people don't want love. And they don't want me."

"Yes!" John's contradiction was emphatic; there was a hint of that fire in his voice suddenly. "At my church! These people have never even had the *choice* of love! They have barely even *heard* of love, from you or anyone else! And it doesn't matter one bit whether they want you or not!

"Do you suppose those people who heard my voice two thousand years ago wanted me? That I preached for some glory of my own? For some reward?"

"They came out to hear you," Cliff defended his point. "You are the glorious evangelist!"

"For *you!*" John fired the pronoun like a missile at Cliff. "For you I am the glorious evangelist. But if I was that in my day for many, for thousands even, there were more thousands who listened but would not hear. On the very banks of the Jordan between Jerusalem and Bethany where I preached for such a brief time, there were those who came and would not hear. In Jerusalem, at the counting tables of the bazaar keepers, in the dining rooms of the comfortable, in the private council chambers of the Jerusalem establishment, among the Doctors of the Holy Law and the Priests of the Holy of Holies, in Judah and in Galilee—people listened to tales of my preaching and did not hear. Throughout all the land—the Beulah Land *my* ancestors spoke about—there were always those who listened and those who didn't, those who heard and those who might as well have had no ears at all.

"But my mission was not to make them hear. My mission was to speak to them, knowing that, whether they chose to hear or not was beyond what was given me to control. My mission was to be the *occasion* for *their* choice between either listening merely, or listening and hearing. My mission was to announce. To reveal. To exhort. To be clear. To let no man and no woman say afterward that I was not plain enough in my words, not direct enough in my speech, not clear enough in my voice, not passionate enough in my spirit.

"Alone, of all the people of that time—except his mother—I knew the Messiah was at hand. I was mindful of my mission. 'Repent!' I shouted that word to all the land. 'The Kingdom of Heaven is at hand! Confess your sinfulness. Be washed clean!'

"There were those around me who said the air turned red with the passion of my soul. And when those who listened to my voice and *heard* what I was saying, when *they* came, I had another message. Clear. Plain. Direct. 'I baptize you with water,' I told them all. 'But one has already come among you who will baptize with fire and the Holy Spirit.'

"And when Jesus himself came out to that bend in the Jordan River where I stood all day preaching and baptizing, again my mission was to be clear, plain, direct. No mistakes! Let the listener hear or not! 'This is the Lamb of God who takes away the sins of the world.' "

All the fire of the Baptist's passion made those words come alive for Cliff as they had never been. But, still, he insisted with a new vehemence, the Baptist not only had a reward, but it was a greater one than Cliff had been talking about before. "What greater reward can there be than to be the one man to baptize Jesus, to see the Holy Spirit above his head, to announce him truly, really, there beside you, as the Lamb of God? Is that not glory? Is that not reward? Have I expected even a fraction of that? By comparison, what reward, what glory, have I sought?"

The Baptist's answer began in a voice of extraordinary command. "Let me tell you about my reward. If you imagine there was glory and satisfaction, let me tell you about my reward.

"I lived for thirty years in a desert that was fit only for camels to cross. I lived for those years far away from parents, family, friends, comfort. When I came to the edges of that world where people lived their normal lives, it was not to join them, but to call them, to rouse them from their torpor, their self-indulgence, their complacency, their conformity to mere mortal law. When I came into the public eye, it was not for my glory or my prominence.

"I could have had prominence, make no mistake. When the delegation from the all-powerful Sanhedrin came out to the Jordan to ask by whose authority I baptized the people, I could have claimed glory and prominence enough for any man.

" 'Are you Elias,' they demanded, 'who will appear in Israel just prior to the arrival of the Messiah?'

"My answer? Just a simple 'No.'

" 'Are you a prophet?' That was the next question. If I had said yes to that, or given even a vague assent, said agreeable things, I could have gone back with them to Jersualem and enjoyed the glory and popularity that men confer on important personages.

" 'No,' I answered. 'I'm not a prophet.' That was the

end of any chance I had of worldly glory. They knew then from my own lips that I was nobody.

"I was clear and direct in telling them who I was. 'I am the voice of one crying in the wilderness. Prepare the way of the Lord!' But that, and anything else I said, meant nothing to those self-important gentlemen. They listened. They did not hear. And they left.

"It was not my prominence that brought me to public attention. It was that I was to be the first to make Jesus prominent. I must decrease, I told my own followers, and he must increase. And that was the clear, plain, direct fact. No mistakes. And no glory. As to the great reward of baptizing him: Yes. The sole joys of my life consisted of the two times when we were near each other. Both times, he came to me. Both times I knew him, though we had not met. The first time, I was in my mother's womb. The second time was thirty years later. He simply appeared then, on the banks of the Jordan. He didn't say, 'I'm the Messiah,' I knew. And he knew. He didn't even say, 'I am Jesus.' He said, 'Baptize me, so that the law may be fulfilled.' And I did.

"Now, you would say, Cliff, once my mission seemed so well and faithfully completed, I might have expected a little consideration. That's the way love should always work, according to you. Love with a return, eh? But, instead, I walked in yet another shadow of Jesus. As I had baptized him with water and thus announced him as the Messiah who would baptize with the Holy Spirit, so I announced his coming death, by being put to death first with the wanton, cowardly consent of King Herod."

There was an immense silence. The clock ticked and

chimed and did not disturb that silence. Cliff had much to absorb. He had not thought about the Baptist in such stark terms. Oh, he knew the facts; but now, to listen to the Baptist himself was to see the very outlines of the Jordan, hear the strident voice of John calling out upon its banks, know the temptation of accepting the comfort of life as a member of the Sanhedrin, see Jesus walking toward him in the early morning sun. And it was, almost, to feel the blade that severed John's head from his shoulders. Cliff shuddered.

"So," he whispered, "I have been wrong to preach of love's reward."

"No." The Baptist's voice was as soft as Cliff's whisper, but it was clear. Always, the Baptist was clear. "Pray in love for love's goodness. Never ask for extreme trials. That would be to tempt God. And it would be pride. It would be to say: 'Try me! Test me. I am strong!' Instead of seeking what you may not be able to sustain, pray rather that God's will be done in you.

"And yet be ready to recognize and seize that moment in which you may be asked to accept such trials. Not as I had to. Not for all your life. Few people are asked to do that. But at some one time or another, most people are called to some extreme of trial they would not, and should not, ask for. They are called to bear for a short time, for a brief moment, what was my whole life's calling: selfless love."

Cliff understood that this was such a time for him. He understood that much. "But," he wanted to be clear, "does selfless love mean that my failure here is something I must accept? Is that selfless love now, here, in this situation? Because, if it is, that's a big relief in a way. Whatever I do here, whether I stay and give in to this crowd, or fight them and get tossed out, I'm defeated."

"Oh, Cliff!" It was a mild censure compared to what he might have expected from this explosive visitor. "The answer to that question depends on what you mean by failure and defeat. And it depends on whose failure and defeat you think you are talking about.

"In the terms you mean, *defeat* is the one word that would summarize my whole life! Except for some six months of my thirty years, I was poor, exiled, alone. When my moment in the glare of notoriety and acclaim had served its purpose, I was killed by a drunken soldier in the dungeon of a palace of a drunken king.

"In the terms you mean, *defeat* is the one word that would summarize the entire life of Jesus. He was poor. He wandered the land with a band of fishermen and the like. He died a horrible death in a manner reserved for criminals and the dregs of society.

"In the terms you mean, *defeat* is in fact the summary of the whole Gospel message.

"And yet, you know as surely as you are alive that none of that was failure and defeat. You know, because you have listened and heard. You know because you have seen that so-called failure in the ambit of God's own vision, as he has revealed it to you. You understand that he uses the weak, the failed, the defeated of this world for his greatest victories, victories that whole armies of successful men could not win.

"No failure, no human defeat that turns out to be a victory for the living God, a victory of his will, can be called a defeat at all.

"And so we come down to the question of whose failure and whose defeat you are worried about. If you have yourself in mind only, then I ask, what is this tremendous weight of importance you attach to yourself? If that is your worry here, then there is no tomorrow whose lasting joy and light will depend on your decision to stay or to leave, on your compromise or your defeat. Simply leave. It won't make any difference.

"But if you tell me that in your decision either to stay and give in, or to fight and be thrown out, it is not you who are defeated, but that it is Jesus' love that is defeated, then that is another matter. If that is truly the case, and there is no doubt in your mind, then a moment of selfless love of Jesus has come to you, been presented to you, been laid in your hands, as surely as such moments came to Peter and James and Andrew. They tasted some joys of love as you have, and they joined them to Jesus' joy. Will you now as willingly take some share in his suffering, if need be? Some part in his sacrifice? For *his* will? *That* is the meaning of selfless love.

"Upon your response to such a moment, and to that question, rest your well-being in truth, and that of the people entrusted to you. For make no mistake: What you decide to do with this moment *can* make a shining difference for all the moments and hours and tomorrows that follow it, and for all the people you serve as Jesus' servant.

"And that brings us to a matter we haven't even mentioned. The people entrusted to you."

It was true. Cliff had been so engrossed in his own painful dilemma, that he had all but forgotten to consider the people whose spiritual welfare had brought him to this crisis. Until now, until this time in the company of the Baptist, he had not understood any part of his mission in terms of selfless love. His thought had been centered on *his* defeat, on the rewards of love slipping from *his* hands. Yet now that he was beginning to see that such moments do come, that one such moment had come for him, he desperately wanted guidance on how to deal with it. Not for himself. Not for his own "return" on love, though he didn't hide the fact that he was still afraid for himself, for his dismal failure, for his own weakness. That, in fact, was precisely why he had to learn how to act for the sake of these people about whom he really did care. They were all like Edna for him now. All abandoned by those who should have watched over them. Abandoned by the Reverend Cliffton B., who should have loved Jesus enough to be—at this time and in this mission and in his own way—as clear, as plain, as direct, as the Baptist had been in his time, his mission, his way.

Nevertheless, there was a final moment of wavering for Cliff. Selfless love is not an easy gift to take in hand, even for a time. He knew, he told John, that if he "whipped the hides off these people with the same verve and violence you used, they'll have my own hide instead, and send me packing, to boot."

John understood the hesitation. There was perhaps no one except Jesus who would understand it better. "They might," he admitted. "But that isn't really the choice you will give them.

"In fact, they will only make a choice at all, in the sense we have been speaking of, if you can give them just one glimpse of that shining promise of love that has been buried for them beneath all the layers of suburban pretensions and flippant sensualities and romantic myths and political gospels. They will make a choice at all only if you can let them glimpse even for one instant the love and the spirit that suffuse and enliven all they do and all their institutions, as blood enlivens their bodies.

"That is why I came to my desert wilderness. That is why you have come to this place. That is the work of an evangelist, in good times and in bad."

"Whether convenient or inconvenient," Cliff finished the thought with the words of St. Paul.

"Exactly so. Just be clear. . . ."

"Yes," Cliff knew by now: "Clear. Plain. Direct."

"And, one thing more." John smiled in parting, "it's love's own guidance you'll be giving them. Remember that there is a long history behind you to affirm that Jesus did come, that he is here: As surely as he walked toward me in that early morning sunlight, he is here. As you can see, you have a little more help than you realized and it is closer at hand than you knew."

❋

Cliff didn't know how long he had spent in the presence of the Baptist. But, when it was over, when around him there were only the accustomed things—the chiming of the clock, the dim sounds of the outside world—he had a clarity of mind and spirit and solidity of purpose that he had never known before.

He knew it didn't matter anymore that, until now, he had misunderstood the words he had read so often in the Gospels, or that he had mistaken the Baptist's role. Love could bypass all those mistakes. Cliff had had no evil intent. His had been only a mortal weakness, and a fear toward end of his brilliant career that he was losing his touch. The Baptist had not come to him in harshness. He

had come to share with Cliff his own love, the most tower-
ing and the purest love given by any man to Jesus.

Cliff did not emerge from his study all night long. By
dawn he had drawn up a long list of names and, before
seven o'clock, he was on the telephone, rousing the members of the council from their sleep and from their
lethargy. He assigned to each one of them a part of the list.
They were, he told them, to call each person and to follow
up with a personal visit, if need be. They were to see to it
that every member of the congregation came to the community auditorium that very evening. No excuses! Not
theirs. Not anyone else's. No prior engagements, no un-
foreseen circumstances short of a fever of 110°, were to
stand in the way.

He was clear. And he was direct. For once, he wanted
each and every member of the congregation—no matter if
they hadn't darkened the door of the church in years—
sitting before him in the auditorium that evening.

Whether it was due to his command or their curiosity
or, perhaps, "a little more help than he realized he had,"
that evening at eight o'clock he strode onto the stage of the
auditorium; and, for the first time in all the wearing, disappointing months he had been at the Church of John the
Baptist, he saw before him every member of his congregation.

He had no notes, and no need of any. He watched the
sea of chattering faces. He was in no hurry to silence them.
He caught stray bits of their conversation that floated up
to him like parts of the atmosphere of the place. "So that's
what the famous Reverend Cliffton B. looks like. . . ."
"Where's his wife . . .?" "What's he mean, calling us all as
though we were children . . .?" "Is he going to resign . . .?"

"Well, you heard about the baptism. . . ." "I'll bet he's leaving and wants to blame us. . . ." ". . . resign. . . ."

Little by little, quiet spread over the hall. Faces turned forward, though less in an attitude of interest than one of reconnoitering, as though to say: "Let's see what you've got."

Cliff began quietly, clearly, his glance and his voice reaching every part of the auditorium: "Hello, strangers."

That brought a laugh. Not a self-conscious one: they took with good grace the criticism buried in such a wry greeting from this man who had been their pastor for close to a year. Some had seen him no more than once at a dinner party, and most had never seen him at all. The laughter died away. Cliff let the expectant silence that came after it grow until his congregation was clearly becoming uncomfortable under his stare.

Finally, he chose to relieve their tension. "I would like to have greeted you all in another way. I would like to have looked upon many a familiar face and said: 'Hello, sisters and brothers in Jesus.' But we have not been that to one another—not even the ones of you that I do know, have been that—" a quick glance at the council, seated in a group near the front.

"I would like to have added to my greeting, 'Hello, my countrymen, my fellow Americans.' That would probably have embarrassed you. But that's not the reason I didn't say those words.

"The fact is that I'm not sure we are fellow Americans —at least not in any sense I have understood in my life."

There were a few glances back and forth among the listeners. The humor was over. That was clear. Better brace themselves, the look said. Maybe he'd make it short, and they could get home in time to catch the ten o'clock news.

"And yet," Cliff continued quickly, silencing the looks and the whispers, "in another sense, I know each one of you strangers sitting out there. I know you because you're perfect copies of one another. And each one of you is almost a perfect copy of me."

Now skepticism replaced impatience.

"Oh, yes," Cliff held up his hand for quiet. "I led you very well. Better than I knew. The place I left in order to come here was quite different from this community. But, when I settled here, I walked along your clean and well-patrolled streets as though I had known them all my life. I took your fine new houses for granted as though they were mine. I delighted in the physical beauty of this place, in the cool breezes. I was your perfect spiritual leader. I knew my sheep, I thought. But the truth was, my sheep knew me better than I knew myself! You all remember what Abe Lincoln said about fooling all of the people some of the time, and some of the people all the time, but not all the people all of the time. Well, I didn't fool you for a minute!

"When I agreed to come here, I told myself I was doing it for you; that I was giving up a post where I was comfortable and loved and could have lived out my days in blessings and contentment with my wife happy at my side, until Jesus would call us home.

"The truth is, though, that without even realizing it, I relished sacrificing all of that. There was a smugness I disguised so well, even I didn't see it. I would let you benefit from my experience, my learning, my skill. I would accept your admiration, and your gratitude. Considering my sacrifice, was that not my due?

"Like every one of you, I had worked long and hard, and had come to claim what I had earned. I came out of pride. I came as a favor to you.

"And yet, my beloved strangers, I have done you no favor. I have visited many of your homes, but I have not brought some special light with me past your thresholds. I visited you because that's the social way of things. When some of you came to me looking for light, for advice, I counseled you in ways I knew would be acceptable to you. I even preached to you—to the few of you who came—in a style geared to *your* own style.

"So, you see, I know you well, my beloved strangers. Not that that's a credit to any of us. I know you the way a machine can know you. You *are* the four-bedroom house where you live. You *are* the nicely paid job you hold. You *are* the social company you keep, the car you drive, the vacations you can—or can't—afford, the security systems that keep you and your stereo sets, and other 'necessities of life' safe from thugs and robbers. You see: I know you well. I know you the way most of you know each other.

" 'Well, so what?' That's the angry question I see in some of yours eyes. 'So what if that's what we like, if that's how we live, if that's what we are? Isn't that what our fathers or uncles or grandfathers came to this country to find? A better life! It's our good luck that we made it. Should we feel guilty, or something? After all, that's the American dream, right?'

"Wrong! That's not the American dream! That may be a nice setting for it, for the moment. But if that's all there is to the dream, then it's no dream at all, but just a cheap fantasy purchased at a very dear price.

"Oh, the fantasy keeps you busy, all right. And it's a

good thing it does. Because I have a feeling that, if you stopped the dinner parties and the dances and the fund raisers and the endless list of busy-life activities, if you simply faced each other without the music and the excitement, you'd find you are to each other exactly what I called you when I began: Strangers."

A murmur of anger and discomfort rippled through the hall, but Cliff didn't wait for silence before going on.

"Not long ago, I had a special reason to stop and think very deeply about the American dream. About my ancestors who came here to find it, to secure it, never doubting its promise. For my family, that saga began nearly four hundred years ago. But it's not the time that matters. Whoever has come here, early or late, has come looking for the same dream, a dream that has never changed. The dream had physical contours: a land entrancing in its beauty, enriching in its resources, sheltering in its strength, consoling in its promise.

"But the dream was more than that. It was more than hunger for land and physical well-being. It was more, because it had a heart and a soul to it. The heart of that dream was hope. That same John Smith who came to these shores in a little boat called the *Susan Constant*—the same one that brought my ancestors here—said once that 'in every hardy hope there is a kernel of love.'

"Love. That was the soul of the dream.

"Every man and woman who has ever come here, has come for that dream, in that hope, to live in that love.

"And yet, nearly everyone in this land looks around now and wonders, 'what has happened to hope? Is it summed up in the brick walls of our fortress-houses that cut us off from one another and from the rest of the world?

And what has happened to love? What has happened to the heart and the soul of the American dream?"

Cliff paused, turning his thoughts inward, mustering the courage he had lacked until now. It took only a moment. Then he went on. Clear. Direct.

"Who hasn't said, or heard someone say, 'There are no frontiers left for us to conquer?' And yet, when I was first approached to come here and be your pastor, I was told that this place is a new frontier in its own way. This community where we all live in greater comfort and security than many a fabled king or queen of past centuries, this is a new frontier. So they told me.

"I thought at the time that was just a romantic figure of speech. But I know better now. Strangers though we are, we stand together in a time and place where choices must be made—are being made even now, each day and week and year. Choices that will dictate the contours of a new world.

"Perhaps that world will be what so many of our opinion makers tell us: A land not only paved, but encased in the hard cement of industrial expansion, dotted with steel structures whose chrome facades reflect the cold, distorted faces of science and technology. A land inhabited by people who are identified by numbers, who live without love, without compassion, with merely passing pleasures, with merely human goals, and without hope that any new day will bring any dream not reflected in those chrome facades. A land whose people owe loyalty to none but themselves, and are destined—in their own minds—to disappear finally from human sight, their bodies disposed of by the most efficient technical means available, their memory preserved in computer files for seven-to-ten years until the statute of limitations runs out, and all else extinguished along with the living blood that once flowed in their veins.

" 'That's not possible here,' we used to say. Yet, now, is there anyone among us who doesn't cringe at the real possibility that such a world is already far along in the making?

" 'So, if it is,' we say, 'what can we do about it? We're caught up in it all like everyone else, as helpless as everyone else. We didn't do it. We don't like it anymore than you do. We can't help it. Some of us will be dead before it arrives!'

"Perhaps, my beloved and intimate strangers! Perhaps. But at every frontier there is a choice to be made. A choice of direction. A choice about which little trails to blaze, which little paths to cut. The portrait of our future which is already etching its outlines in this land and carving its way into our lives, is not the only choice or the only path.

"Until now, the strange and wonderful strength of the American dream has shimmered on the horizon, a shining promise of a land and a life offered to us by God himself. But now, we are crossing a new frontier. And we all have a new choice to make. It is a choice about belief. But, at its core, the choice does not concern political beliefs. Nor does it concern social values. At its core, this is a choice about love and hope, caring, and compassion. And it is a choice that will decide the future of this land as surely as the choices made by our forefathers decided our existence today.

"In this land, we have always understood that if we were to have justice and hope, our laws alone would not be enough. In this land, there has always been a consensus that, if our laws would embody and enshrine our hopes, they would have to have their origin and fulfillment in the guarantee of God. 'One nation, under God,' we have always said. Even on Mammon's exchange, on our money, we did not give fealty to Caesar, but to God.

"How could that be? What did we mean when we said 'one nation, under God'? Did we not mean that all our laws, our customs and our dealings with one another must reflect, must take part in, some divine purpose in our lives? Did we not mean to heed the words of Moses when he told the people to observe the commandments of the Lord and thus give evidence of their wisdom and intelligence to all the nations surrounding them? Did we not mean that we had seen clearly in other lands how law and custom that were *not* based on the simple command to love God and neighbor became heavy chains that held such nations fast in dungeons of helplessness and hopelessness? Did we not all break those chains when we came here? Did we not all vow never to be put in such chains again? Have we not for centuries now lived and died in the knowledge that, apart from God, apart from our love for him and for our neighbors, there is no help, no dream, no hope, no promise, no Beulah Land?

"As we cross this new frontier, if we are persuaded to leave behind that understanding, if we discard the hope that has been guaranteed us by the life and death and resurrection of one man who was God, then we will no longer see our reflection as a nation or as individuals in the portrait he has drawn so clearly for us. If we are persuaded that love is too fragile a thing to serve us in this hard world, and that there is in the reality of our time no guarantor of love any longer, then we will surely see our reflection only in the hard chrome facades of our buildings and our lives.

"Why? Because no amount of socializing, of sociologizing, of social do-gooding, and endless lawmaking, *ensures* love. And no amount of politicking ensures the *hope* of love.

"You see, my beloved strangers, it works the other way around. The surety, the guarantees we look for, lie in love. It is love that guarantees the success of our social order. It is our social order based on love that guarantees our laws. It is only God himself who has guaranteed love. And it is Jesus, God's son, who has given us that unending promise.

"If you think that those words sound soft and unrealistic in this tough and secular world, think again. Think *again*! They are the truest, hardest, most uncompromising words this world has ever heard. Jesus died on a cross for those words. Men and women through the ages have lived and died by and for those words. Here and now, in this time and place, if you dare to say those words aloud, you had better be strong enough to bear the scorn of many, and still stand tall and say clearly, directly, that word: Love!

"Suppose for a moment that every one of us here in this hall, and everyone beyond these walls—our judges, our lawmakers and our bankers and our business tycoons, and our gurus of every kind and sort—were to shout the two commands of love: 'Love the Lord thy God, and love thy neighbor as thyself.' Can anyone of us imagine that injustice would survive such a revolution? If we lived by those two laws of love, would we need fortress-homes? Would we pollute our land? Would we kill each other in our streets and poison one another with drugs? Would we strip ourselves of all identity except what is useful to the money changers and tax collectors? Would we do the thousands of things that separate us from each other, and that make us enemies fighting over the scraps that fall from the tattered dream of love and hope that originally brought us all here?

"If we in this generation, the first waves of Americans to cross the new frontier, walk into the nightmare of the so-called brave new world, it will be because we have been too cowardly to stand beneath the banner of love, too weak in our fears to shout love's name as the only guarantee of hope in our lives and in our land. It will be because we say: 'All right, we lay down our banner. We step aside from our dream.' It will be because we say: 'All right, banish Love and hope from all quarters of our public and private lives. Banish observance of Love's commandments. Erase the American dream. Bequeath this land to graft and corruption and conformity and to the pollution not merely of our rivers and streams and reservoirs and earth, but of our minds, our hearts, our souls.' "

There was no sound of whispers when Cliff paused for a moment. There were no glances of derision. There was no doubt that they all stood on the very frontier he described, or that they were engaged, willy-nilly, in the choice that he had described as the overriding issue of this day.

When he spoke again, it was in a voice so calm it almost belied the struggle he had himself come through only one night before this one. "In the months I have been with you, I have given you no reason not to say: 'All right, we surrender our banner of Love.' I have given you no reason not to step aside from the dream that has gathered us all as one people in this land. Do you know what I have been for you? I have been exactly what you asked me to be: a social bowknot in a purely secular community. I became like so many of my clerical friends who turned into pastors and preachers of a social gospel, chaplains of whatever vogue or cause that swept their way.

"I wonder if you can ever know how easy it is to surrender to those pressures. It seems so effective, so popular, so attractive. Even in this little community it brings one into the comfort of public acclaim, into the company of the powerful, into the power-lines of civil authority. But now I know how empty and troubled that surrender leaves a person who has been given, not civil, but moral authority, and whose only power must lie in the order of spirit.

"If I surrender, if I preach to you of social gospels and political interests, then the moral and spiritual foundations upon which this community—as every community in America—depends, will crumble. So, here we stand. You and I, engaged in a great, troubling choice about which path to choose as we cross this new frontier. An awesome choice. A very clear choice.

"One path is marked by belief in Jesus, by cultivation of his love, by nourishment in the hope only he gives.

"The other—the only other one available—is marked by the signs of total secularism, total de-Christianization of homes, schools, cities, states, every state in the Union itself. These are the only two paths opening out from this frontier place. No other choices!

"Now, I could leave you here at the joining of these two ways. I could walk away and ignore you, murmuring and resentful of my attitude, perhaps; fearful for your future, certainly; bewildered probably; and definitely disappointed. And you would have a right to be all of those things; because I am, after all, still your pastor, and you are the people of God, the people of my congregation. I owe you a debt. Here and now, listen to me as I pay that debt of my duty in your regard.

"Last night, I chose one of those paths. I made my own personal choice. I chose the path followed by the greatest man ever born of woman. John the Baptist. I am pastor of the church named after him. He loved Jesus supremely. He believed in Jesus. He hoped in Jesus. I—if I am to be any good at all—must imitate John. And, so I have chosen the first of those two paths: belief and hope in Jesus, observance of his commandments of love, inheritance of a courage that is unimaginable without love as its ground and base.

"In practical terms, here and now, what does this choice of mine mean?

"It means this: I will be your pastor, leading you in reproducing the role of Jesus in your daily lives. I will not imitate you anymore. I'll do my best to follow the style and the mind of the person I work for. You only *pay* me. He employs me! I work for Jesus. I won't celebrate his role in your lives like the MC in a series of outdoor jamborees. Across the plaza, then, that's his sacred place in the community: his church. That's the only reason for its being there. Oh yes, all things and every place belong to him. He is everywhere. But the church is his sacred shrine. If we abandon that special place of his, we get away from all understanding of what the words *sacred* and *blessed* mean in this world. For his presence is not the same everywhere. Certain places are sanctified and consecrated to him in a special manner. Our church is one such place.

"In practical terms, this choice of mine means that Jesus will be the centerpiece of this church. The church will be the centerpiece of the congregation. His love will be the centerpiece of all I do. Mine for him. Mine in him for you. The Baptist said he came to prepare the way of our Lord Jesus. Every pastor must come prepared to do the same, not asking or expecting anything in return except to serve him. Everyone who follows such a pastor must know he is following our Savior. And together, as pastor and people, we must be confident that we will find our way, because we have a Savior who has gone before us into all of our tomorrows.

"And again, in practical terms, the choice I've made means that I will no longer be a dispenser of social glue. I will be your pastor, if you want me and for as long as you want me. But I will preach to you about Jesus, who is love. I will preach to you of the courage and the justice and the caring and the hope that are love's children. I will welcome you to his holy place, his church. I will baptize your children there. I will marry your youngsters there. And, there, I will commend your souls to the heart of love, when you die. I will do all those things in the place he has provided and made holy by his special presence.

"In practical terms, that choice of mine means that as your pastor, I will say to you all: Please come with me. But come prepared! Come equipped with an eye for God's hidden graces. Come with a new instinct for the inventions of his love. Come with a deep conviction that this Lord, this Jesus, this God, who became man while remaining God, that this loving savior of ours outweighs all the hard facts of our human living. He will make up for any nostalgia we may feel for the sweetness of former ways. He will smother even the littlest flicker of despair or discouragement in the warm liquid power of his love.

"And be sure to come with a sense of dreaming, of aspiring, of envisioning, that goes beyond the stretch of pavement outside your house. Make sure that you have ample supplies of that durable, unbeatable patience with which Americans first faced that long, hard route to their promised Beulah Land. And, in the name of God and for the glory of our lord, Christ Jesus, be prepared to live your lives as the community of his chosen ones and the associates of his saints and the bearers of his love. 'Humbly welcome the word that has taken root in you. Act on this word. If all you do is listen to it, you are deceiving yourselves.'

"That is what my choice means, in practical terms.

"And so, we come to your turn. Your choice. If you choose to make of Jesus a little myth, and a social leader out of his pastor, then you will have chosen the second path facing you at this new frontier. And you will not find me on that path. Nor as pastor in this church. That is a choice that need not wait upon the completion of my first year. You will make the choice here tonight. You will make it, because now it has been put to you. Clearly. Directly. And there is not one person listening to me now who can say, 'I have not heard.' There is no one who can say, 'Whatever happens, it is not my doing.' "

Cliff looked around at his listeners one last time. Then, clearly and directly, he described for them the simple and undramatic manner in which he would cross tomorrow's frontier.

"I will," he said, "leave this community hall. I will walk the few dozen yards across the plaza to our church. I

invite you—all of you, any of you—to follow me there. It
will be your choice. If you do not come to join me there,
then that will be your answer. But if you do, know that
you and I will be together for one reason, and that from
this night forward in all our meetings and celebrations, in
all our sorrows and joys, in everything, I will keep saying,
as David did: Glorify the Lord with me!"

❋

Cliff didn't know how long he waited, Julia by his side,
in the deep silence of the church. It was not as easy a time
as he had spent with the Baptist the night before. He low-
ered his head and covered his face with his hands. He let
his mind travel over last night's scenes: "These people
never had the choice of love . . . My mission was to be the
occasion for their choice . . . Clear. Plain. Direct. No mistakes. And no glory . . . Defeat is the one word that would
summarize my whole life . . . Defeat would summarize
the life of Jesus. . . ." It was all prayer, a prayer of presence
and contemplation. It conveyed such sweetness to him that
Cliff felt Jesus was preparing him with consolation, for the
failure of his appeal to his congregation.

He must have been completely absorbed, for it was
only Julia's gentle voice and the soft touch of her hand
that roused him. When he raised his head to look at her,
and saw tears streaming down her cheeks, his first thought
was that he had been selfish again, had thought only of
himself again. He leaned forward to speak to her, to con-
sole her. But, even at the sight of her tears, he suddenly
realized that she was smiling, too.

It was only then that Cliff became quietly aware that
the church was filling up. By twos and threes and fives, his

congregation was coming to Jesus at the invitation of his selfless servant. He watched as the people filled the pews, crowded into the aisles and the sanctuary. He watched, and he felt oceans of pain recede from his spirit, felt full rivers of hope flood his soul. And still he watched, until the last stragglers were wedged in, and there was quiet.

At last, he mounted the steps to the pulpit where he belonged, and welcomed the congregation of John the Baptist to the farther shores of Heaven's tableland.

There Is Still Love

THE SUREST EFFECT of love in an individual is an increase of what we all recognize as happiness. It is unmistakable. When we love, and are loved, that happiness is irrepressible in us. Like fresh spring water, it bathes everything within us and spills out into our lives. It seeks to splash and sparkle and wash the world about us until everything in and around us reflects a new light.

The surest effect of love's withdrawal or of separation from a loved one is an equally unmistakable and painful yearning.

So unmistakable are the effects of love, and so universal is its touch, that love may be the only nonmaterial, unmeasurable thing in our universe about which there is no argument. It is there. It is real. Everyone wants it. Nobody denies its desirability. Its effects are of immense force in our personal lives. Its presence or its absence can transform an individual, a family, a block, a neighborhood, a city, a nation. It affects our perception; and it affects what is perceived. The greater the love, the greater its effects until, ultimately, at love's greatest height, at its highest intensity and its most sublime constancy, even death itself cannot hold out against it.

As Christians, we have always believed that God is the source and origin of love, as of all things. That all things, in fact, were created with love by Love's hand. And we have always believed that Jesus Christ, who is God, walked among us and, in doing so, formed for us a bridge across a gap that separated us from Love, a chasm that we could not have crossed alone in our unaided weakness. That bridge, we believe, spans all time and all space. That bridge, we believe, was not only constructed for us by Jesus, but itself is made of everything he was and everything he did. In his miracles, in his parables, in all his life of minutes and hours and days and years as a man, as God in human form, he revealed the essence, the true nature, the meaning, and the source of love, and opened its pathways to us. In his conception in the womb of the Virgin. In his birth as a human infant. In his labors. In his suffering. In his death. In his resurrection, his body transfigured then in inchangeable glory. In his rising from the presence of those mortal men and women to whom he had been closest on earth, to return to his Father. In all of that, he revealed to us more than had ever been known of love, of love's reason, and of love's promise. More than that! He revealed Love itself in its totality—if we have the mind to understand, the clarity of spirit to see.

In all of that, he prepared the way for us to possess and be possessed by Love here and now, to live with it, to mold our mortal lives however imperfectly in Love's image; and, finally, to possess and be possessed by Love completely and to live Love perfectly with him when our mortal lives are done.

That, we believe, is the meaning, the purpose, and the goal of our lives. That is Love's unchanging vision.

Once our lives are brushed with even the lightest touch of that vision, with the most imperfect understanding of that meaning, once we see the barest outlines of Love's purpose, we cannot bear to let it go. Everything changes for us. That is why, in my mind and in my prayers for Laura M. and all the others whose stories I have told in this book, I have added the ending that, in Love's name, I pray will be theirs. In Love's name, I have pictured a transformation that is there for them, because Jesus lived among us and because he built that bridge to Love, and because he invited us to cross that bridge with him to Love's home.

In every age and in every place, there have always been other invitations, other visions. The missionaries of those other visions have always been loud and strident and persuasive. They have always cried out to us with an energy that is remarkable, beckoned to us, their hands filled with glittering rewards. Pleasure. Safety. Gold. Power. Dominion. Sovereignty. Authority. Empire. All or some of those mixed in an alchemistic brew. "Drink it," they have invited, "and our vision of happiness will be yours. The world, and all its promise besides, will be yours."

It is easy to understand invitations like that. So powerful, so filled with lure, so here-and-now are they, that the gospel records Jesus himself was approached by his archenemy, Satan, bearing just those promises: The temptations of Jesus. "All this and more will I give you. . . ."

Today, in our age, the promise is a different one. It is dour and stark and bleak. It is a promise emptied of all the glitter and lure. Yet its missionaries are as filled with zeal as if they were offering all the never-ever rainbows arching at the end of all the most terrible storms of life. As if they bore for us a meaning and promise and vision so tantalizing that, if only we would listen, if only we would drape our lives with the cloak of that meaning and that promise, we would be transformed forever, and our world would be a far different place.

In that much, of course, they are right. Our world would be a far different place.

They are clear, these new missionaries. No waffling weakens their conviction. No objections deter them from their message or their mission of persuasion.

"You say your origins and ours are in love," they chide us. "But we know better. Your origins and ours lie in a bucketful of mud. From blind, impersonal matter. Blind impersonal matter holds this universe together in harmony. Blind, impersonal matter: That is the way and the truth and the reality.

"You say you were created in the image and the likeness of God, and by the hand of Love," these missionaries continue their sermon. "But we know better. Take it or leave it: Mud was your mother and an awesome animal was your father.

"You say your meaning is contained and expressed in what you call your soul with its will and its intellect, and that this soul is filled with a yearning for God, and that you are thus a single, unique person. We know better nowadays. Your meaning as a person is that of a thing that starts off as a baby outside the womb—before that it was an impersonal blob; forever, after emerging from your mother, you are a bundle of behaviorisms and compulsions. The 'you' you are is a clever collection of instincts and movements tied together like a bundle of sticks. And we know how to train that bundle, restrain it, restructure it, tinker with it in a thousand clever intelligent ways with our ever new rituals—our tests with pigeons and rats and hamsters, our therapies and drugs for memory, sexuality, violence, for everything. And just as we can help solve the painful mystery of 'crib' deaths in infants by studying baby seals, so we can solve the problem of infanticide by parents through our studies of baboons and wild African dogs. And so for all human problems. It's all the same.

"So much," these missionaries tell us, "for your meaning as a person. Now, your meaning as a member of the community can be known and summed up for all to see in exact numbers and ciphers. There are so many of us nowadays (but we can fix that too; just wait) that the most efficient way to deal with you is by the gross, with measurements, norms, rules. Your family must consist of 1.2 children. We must graph your food intake, your tax contributions, your life expectancy, your economic brackets, your politics, your social classifications.

"We draw your portrait, not from the palette of Michelangelo on the ceiling of the Sistine Chapel, but in electronic games. Robotron 2084, for example, is our portrait of the Last Human Family. See yourselves: blond-haired Mom; blue-suited Dad plodding along with his briefcase; little towheaded Mikey. All in danger of perishing at the hands of fearful beings called Grunts, Spheroids, Hulks, Tanks, Brains. And see your salvation: a tiny, white-suited figure in glowing glasses, Robotron 2084! A robot so advanced that it is far superior even to us, its creators. You say that your salvation lies in Love's hands? What robot ever loved? No. Your salvation depends on our brilliance to create machines of even greater brilliance.

"Now," these missionaries proceed at an efficient pace, moving us step by step toward their prize, "now that you know where you came from, and know the accurate profile of yourself, you will appreciate the wisdom with which we propose to govern you and regulate your life.

"It is so simple now. The letter of our law is not clouded by moral right or wrong. Guilty? Or not guilty? According to the law. That's all we ask. Cleverness and brilliance are the measures of the arguments. No vague religious universe is needed as law's foundation, nor is compassion needed for government's rule. Our law does not acknowledge faith, nor does it need to take love's justice into account. For our purposes, it works, and that's what matters, isn't it? It has its little imperfections, we admit, such minor details as that, for instance, we do not yet know what a person is (but we'll fix that, too; just wait).

"Now we are coming close to the prize, the reward of faith. Be patient! Just one more thing before that. All religions must deal with destiny. Your destiny, you have believed, was to die and finally end up with God and his saints and angels in Heaven; or, if you were to be punished, to reside in a painful place called Hell. But we know better. We tell you as sons and daughters of mud and animals your destiny is clear: Disintegration. Like rocks and animals and plants that come from the same primeval slime, we are destined to disintegrate, and to join all the other meaningless particles rushing around the universe, rushing with our cold brothers, the boulders, toward our fiery sisters, the stars.

"And so, at last, we come to our reward for faith in this

new religion. Its glorious promise to you is this: Acceptance. Believe! And you will be accepted by us, the new missionaries. Believe and you will be acclaimed as acolytes of the opinion makers of our day. Accept this trinity of slime, impulses, and disintegration, bow down before it, know the truth, and we will call you enlightened and you will have our blessing.

"Reject this truth, this trinity, however, and you will suffer scorn and derision. Men and women will laugh at your stupidity and move along without you. You will be left embarrassed in our wake, and you will have no part in our acclaim."

That is the catechism and the promise of the missionaries of our day. They labor with vast dedication to fashion a new world, and a new vision with which to comprehend that world. The incantation with which that world and that vision is heralded, is not the ancient 'Holy! Holy! Holy!' of the prophet. It is an incantation of lovelessness and impersonal mechanization. It is chanted in a place where all religious expression—except this single one—is banished from public life.

For, believe you me, this is a new religion, and its propagandists and defenders are true missionaries who propose an entirely different religious belief. The public squares of this new world must be naked, sterilized of contamination by the crucifix. Our comings and our goings are not to be protected any longer by the sacred canopy of Christianity. There is no room for Jesus. Love has no resting place here. And the incantation that is wrung from the very depths of sadness is heard everywhere the new missionaries succeed: Is there still love?

Christians, however, have always been a stubborn lot.

We have been threatened with worse than this. We have been told worse things than these unloving lies about our origins and our destiny. We have been offered far happier prizes than slime and disintegration, Heaven knows, to lure us from that bridge where we follow Jesus. Fortunately, we have always had our Chaplains and our Cliffton B.'s.

And yet we are affected. We are not immune. We live, and work and suffer and love and marry and bear children, grow old and feeble, and die in the same world as everyone else. Are we to wail: "Is there still love?" Are we to try to prove, in some monumental argument with these missionaries, what faith alone supplies when feeble senses fail?

Or, are we rather to live in the sure knowledge of God that is called faith, and that has outlived all the false prophets and all the false answers? Shouldn't we, rather, enter this new and seemingly loveless age protected by the certainty and the courage that only love confers?

There are very few, I suppose, who would deny that the astronauts have stood at the farthest edges of this loveless time and at the very boundaries of our knowledge and our technology. They have reached deeper into our universe than anyone else. They have undergone the most rigorous physical, mental, psychological training and testing ever devised by man. They have attained the highest standards of mind, psyche, and body powers. They all are heroes who have taken the farthest steps into tomorrow. They have lifted off Earth and have entered the totally alien stretches of space.

And by the time they returned, they had discovered that all their technical prowess and physical excellence were as nothing compared to the stunning realization that the only thing distinguishing them from the particles of matter streaming around them in space was love. Only love kept them from becoming nothing but blind, soulless particles.

They had started their journey, each of them, as the most perfect and polished athletes and scientists. Reaching for the outer limits of the cosmos, they unexpectedly touched the hem of Love's garment and they did not withdraw from it. For, they knew: Only Love makes our world a human world. They knew: With Love we can do all they did, travel even out among the alien stars and galaxies—out from Earth that moves in an orbit of some 93 million miles around the sun, in full sight of Sirius, Alpha Centauri, and Procyon and other stars that are merely "dim bulbs" in their distances from us; out along our galaxy, the Milky Way, with its 200 billion stars; out, even further, into what is called the Local Group of Galaxies; and, from there, into the Local Supercluster of Galaxies with its radius of some 100 million light-years; and, from there, out into what astronomers call the universe, a place that contains at least 100 billion galaxies. Only with love can we finally sustain ourselves as we penetrate all that, we and our descendants.

Everywhere we humans go we will carry that atmosphere of love peculiar and necessary to us as human beings whom God created and so loved that He sent his only son Jesus into our world, Earth, so that we, by believing in him, should be saved from becoming blind and soulless particles, mere brothers to the boulders, sisters to the stars.

Well, all of that is fine for astronauts; but most of us will never touch that particular hem of Love's garment. We'll still be down here among the boulders, looking up at the stars, being measured and fitted for a loveless world. What do we do? What is our answer to these new missionaries and to their opinions about us? How can we be expected to find love or give love in a world where every glance falls upon the very opposite?

The single, simple answer to those questions reveals the very strength and the complete fragility of our human condition, of our humanness: We are totally dependent on Love in order merely to be and to remain human. Yet, by merely being human, we partake of what Jesus is: His divine nature.

Our participation in God's life—for that is what human life is destined for—did not begin in a primeval soup or a bucket of slime. It began in a far-off time whose details are only hinted at in the story of a primordial choice. It began in a world in which each man and woman would, by God's own desire, freely choose to love him or not love him.

That choice, at least, is something we can understand. When we desire to be loved, we want that love to be given freely. The choice must be there. An essential element in the joy of hearing those we love say: "I love you!" is the knowledge that they have chosen to say it; that they have chosen us. The choice must be there. God is not like *us* in this matter. *We* are like *God*. We have this trait from Him, because He made us in *his* image.

And so it began, hidden now in the mists of far-off time. In the garden of God's own love, there was that first choice between "Thy will be done" and "My will be done." The very same choice that, for decades, Chaplain saw marching across his campus, has marched across all the millennia of human existence.

A friend of mine, a doctor who is truly devoted to his work, says he is an atheist. When I asked him why he became a doctor, why he sacrificed himself so unsparingly for his patients, he told me, his voice trembling with disgust: "Somebody's got to step in and do something, however small, to help people get through this mess of a world. I do my little bit. But don't speak to me about love, or about a God of love creating this junkyard of suffering and death. Why, we're worse off than the animals, and far more cruel, and much more stupid. Animals don't mug each other. They're not drunken drivers killing over fifty thousand people a year on the roads in this country."

As my doctor friend requested, I didn't tell him about our God of Love creating a world in which there is suffering and death. He has his own will for God, my friend does, and one day when he calms down, we may talk about that. His will for God is that God create a perfect world. But a Christian, a follower of Jesus, has a different anthropology.

It is an anthropology in which that ancient choice about love and will is the only one that, like it or not, is made throughout history by every man and woman. It is an anthropology in which the most anciently given response to that choice was, "My will, not thine, be done." It is an anthropology in which that choice set the course of all that followed. It is an anthropology in which temptation has its say and evil has won its way, by human choice, into the fabric of the universe and the course of our daily lives. It is an anthropology that depends first and foremost and finally on a baby born in Bethlehem, and is crowned by his suffering and death in perfect love on a felon's cross at Calvary. The Cradle and the Cross: the frame of our Christian anthropology.

The new missionaries of slime and disintegration are right about one thing, though: They warn us that we will be laughed at and scorned, if we do not speak and believe as they do. And when I do talk to my doctor friend about Christian anthropology, he will laugh. He's heard it before, of course, and laughed before. But perhaps one day, like Laura and Joan and Karen and Michael and the others, a certain grace will touch him, will invite him to see just once that he, my learned and beloved atheist doctor, has done what he accuses me of doing. He has created a fictional god according to his own requirements, and then has snorted in derision because the God who is Love has not done things as my friend presumes He should have.

Just as there is a Christian anthropology, so too, there is a Christian psychology. It is a psychology according to which, in my mortal flesh, I have reason for my hopes to surmount my weakness and to live forever. My Christian psychology tells me, I do not have to do everything in the lonely isolation of this mortal prison, and that life is not death row. It tells me that God can hear the cry of my weakness, can dry my tears, desires my love, wants my friendship, wants me. That he took all of this upon himself, when he constructed that timeless bridge: when he entered this world of time and space, walked, slept, talked, pained, died, and then rose from death.

Mine is a psychology of love according to which God, too, loved, and had special friends, and has asked for my love and friendship. It is a psychology that depends on one fact: I could not know any of this, or hope for any of this,

or imagine any of this, even in my most sensitive yearn-
ings, unless God had become truly human, so that I could
be fully human and therefore share in his divine glory. He
shared my mortal weakness so that I share his immortal
glory.

Now, there is a very practical side to this Christian
psychology. It is my psychology, after all, and yours. We
walk around. We work. We eat. We sleep. We talk. We
think of this, want that, like or dislike another thing.
Memories cause us grief and joy. My whole life is played
out, as is yours, in a web of thought and wish and hope,
desire, and remembrance.

In Christian psychology, all of that is the active, ongoing picture, the very reflection, of my soul, and of yours.
Christian psychology encompasses all of the ways we perceive and react to the here-and-now world in which we
must live and in which we choose our friends and find our
loves. But it does not end with that world, with our senses
and our imagination and our little wills. It faces all of
reality, and does not demand that any part of reality, visible or invisible to the eye or to our human minds, be cut
off from our day-by-day living. It does not shave off parts of
reality that do not fit a preconceived theory.

With the fullness of perception and sensitivity of our
beings, we know each other; we cultivate one another as
friends, or ignore one another; we abide with one another
as distant acquaintances, or as beloved friends. And we also
know and abide with Jesus either as a distant acquaintance
or as a beloved friend. We cultivate Jesus, or we ignore
him.

If we ignore Jesus and refuse the offer of his friendship,
then, as with any offer of friendship we refuse, we cut

ourselves off from participation in his company. If our desire is to accept his offer of friendship, then, as in any friendship, we must cultivate it. We must find ways to be with him, to draw closer to him, to invite him to be with us, to provide occasions of special closeness, and to make him welcome when he comes.

That decision to ignore Jesus or to seek and cultivate his friendshp is yet another variation on the age-old choice that God offers: His will is to be with us. That is why he came. Our lives are filled with occasions, with moments, in which we either welcome him or walk away from him.

Each man and woman whose story I have told in this book has lived many such moments. Whether any of them will seize upon one of these occasions, will enter into the friendship and company of Jesus in reality, as I have tried to show they can, is their choice. Only theirs. His offer is unchanging and forever.

Of course, it does seem easier for us to know how to go about cultivating real flesh-and-blood friends. We're taught how to do that from our earliest years. We learn to talk and laugh with friends, share and compare experiences with them, invite them to our homes, visit with them in theirs. Can we do that with Jesus?

Yes, we can. Many of us do, all the time. We just don't think of it in the same way. Chaplain lived his entire life cultivating the friendship of Jesus.

In fact, not only can we cultivate friendship with Jesus, but friendship with him alters forever the nature and the quality of every other friendship in our lives. That is what Chaplain wanted so much for his young friend, Joan C., to begin to understand: Our friendships with one another are invitations of Jesus' friendship to us. It is his friendship for us, his love living always for us, that makes love possible between us and other people.

In practical terms, what does cultivating Jesus mean? We don't all find Mary Magdalene waiting for us in our living rooms. We can't all wake up in a dream to find John the beloved disciple by our beside; or walk with the bride and bridegroom of Cana into a time that is miraculously recreated before our eyes; or visit with some beloved friend who lives now in Jesus' presence, as Ed D. did; or talk the night hours away with John the Baptist, as Reverend Cliff did.

The details may be different. The occasions vary. But the ways we have at our disposal to know Jesus, to know about him and who he is and what pleases and displeases him—to cultivate him—such ways are endless in our ordinary lives. When I speak of keeping the company of Jesus, of seeking his love and friendship, I don't mean merely going to church on Sundays, tithing, taking part in church activities, reading the Bible, saying prayers morning and evening. All that presumably I'll do in the measure that I should. The love and friendship that I need is nourished by those things; but the company of Jesus I speak of now is something over and above that.

It is truly a life, a new life, an inner life—inner to me, I mean—spent with Jesus. There is a quiet, wordless, intangible process by which I share the whole web of my active, ongoing life, my whole mind that is the reflection of my soul, with Jesus. I want Jesus to share all of it. I want him to be with me on all the highways and byways of that continuous scene that is myself in action, awake or asleep. I want him to share it all with me. And he wants to share it all. "Behold," he said to me through his beloved friend,

John the Apostle, "I stand at the door and knock. If anyone will open to me, I will enter in, and I will be his friend, and I will never leave him." I have taken Jesus at his word.

This is the inner life I desire. Like Job, "I have made a covenant with my eyes" to see him everywhere, to find him, to let him participate in all I do and in all I am.

Once I admit him to my life, immediately a whole gamut of things becomes clearer and clearer to me. Like Laura M., I can no longer use love for some other end. Like Joan C., I can no longer make "Why not?" my rule and my command to action. Adultery, vengeance, lying, hate, and all the things that are hateful to Love become hateful and painful to me. In all the bad and painful things that happen to me in my life, I will no longer be willing to surrender to lovelessness.

When my brother died not long ago, I went to the doctor who had received him in the hospital and tended him till the end. I wanted to know every detail, all my brother had said, all he had suffered, all the doctor had done and thought and decided—everything about how my brother had died. I wanted to know all that because I loved my brother. It was love that prompted me to seek all the details of his last hours. I knew him better and I loved him more for his courage, for his pain. It was love that did that for me.

And it was to Jesus and his love that I offered my own pain at losing my brother; I shared it with Jesus, as I want to share all in my life with him. He has offered to share it. He came into this world to share it. And, again, I take him at his word. In all my suffering, I take him at his word. I offer him the spittle of hate cast upon my cheek. I offer him the loveless stare of one who cheated me. I suffer things he never suffered, as all of us do—an appendectomy, a difficult birth, the dishonesty of a business partner, the gnawing bite of cancer, humiliations, abandonments, people who hate my skin color, my politics, my religion, my success. Each thing I suffer is peculiar to me. He wants me to make that suffering his, to join it with his, to make it more than mere groaning, to let him transform it by his own revivifying, redeeming grace into part of his own sacrifice. If, at such moments, I must give selfless love, love without a "return," as Reverend Cliff was called upon to do, then I must make that selfless giving his.

And all the good and joyful things that happen to me in my life will no longer be tiny and transient and unimportant. As in my suffering, so in my happiness, I take Jesus at his word. In every act of love, I must implicitly adore him. In my marriage, I must recognize the human parallel to God's completeness, and in my children, the creation that issues from it. Each act that brings me joy, each moment that makes me glad, I offer to him.

Now, all of this is part of Christian psychology. All of this active inner life of sharing is possible only in the fullness of a psychology that does not cut itself off from what it does not understand. The worldly effects of this active friendship with Jesus are as vast, specific, and irreplaceable as they are obvious.

One example. If I offer my pain at betrayal to Jesus, and I offer it with love, I am unlikely to perform an act of vengeance. If millions of us do that, the practical power of vengeance in the world is significantly reduced. If I then actively look for love's meaning in such situations, and act that meaning out in my own life, I have replaced vengeance with love's reply. If millions of us do that, then we lay before our world the same challenge Reverend Cliff laid before his world as it stood on the brink of loveless-ness. If we do that, we may offer the Judson K.'s of our lives—as Matthew Lovely would have, somehow may have advised Ed D. to do—the means to pull back from the greed and destructiveness and emptiness of the purely bottom-line mentality, whether it be in business account-ing or in the awesome business of peacekeeping and peace-making between the nations on Earth.

But beyond the worldly possibilities of the Christian mode of thinking and acting—this Christian psychology—lies a much greater value, an irreplaceable and, for us, an incalculable effect.

As Jesus joins every act of suffering we offer him, to his own perfect suffering, and as he joins every act of love and joy and happiness to his own perfect love and joy and happiness, so it happens that, in uniting ourselves with him in this active life of friendship and love, we are asking him to bring us, our very selves, to himself, in his perfect glory. That is the goal of all our efforts, the desire of all our days, the promise that love offers. Thus we will enter into his glory forever.

Oh, yes, I know: All of this Christian psychology busi-ness is a far cry from that bundle of sticks our newest missionary friends are so busy measuring, that they are so ready to train and modify and restrain and restructure. And I know they jeer at this psychology that is fashioned so that Love's glory may be mine, and so that I may live, however imperfectly, some part of that glory here and now on Earth. But, jeer as they will, they make no promise of life or love to me—not here and now, not ever. I will not trade Love's vision for a bucket of primordial slime. And I will not surrender Love's promise for their guarantee of disintegration.

And, really, though it doesn't matter finally, I don't believe these latter-day missionaries can keep even that bleak, dark promise of theirs. In my inner friendship with Jesus, I must answer them that we are, each one of us, created by Love in Love's image. Nothing in the image of God can disintegrate, can cease to exist. They cannot, we cannot, even imagine nothingness. Not really. We don't know in detail what happened to Judas after he killed himself. (In our mortal fear, most of us probably don't want to know.) But Jesus didn't speak of him as though he had ceased to be. He spoke of him as separated from Love forever. No one knows what that means in the ultimate and final sense. Not even the missionaries of the loveless vision of slime and disintegration know; yet they, too, live in the world as part and parcel of God's creation. They may not seek friendship with God; but, as in all the millennia past, and in all the millennia to come, that is their choice and our choice to make, one by one by one.

This, then, is the anthropology, the psychology, the sacred history of man and woman that we must keep firmly in the forefront of our minds and our lives. This is the word of God revealed through the Holy Spirit of Jesus. This is the arsenal and the strategy of Love. This is Love's unchanging and eternal offer to each of us made even as the evil, the defect, the disorder introduced long ago into the harmony and beauty of God's creation continues in our universe. For the struggle between Jesus and the old enemy continues. Jesus achieved our redemption; but we must choose it freely, saying, as he did: "Thy will, not mine, be done." And so it will continue, this sacred history, until the Last Day when the heavens "will be rolled up like an old parchment, and the Earth will shiver on its foundations, and the mountains melt into dust before the coming of the Lord."